INTERNATIONAL DEVELOPMENT IN FOCUS

Youth Employment Programs in Ghana

Options for Effective Policy Making and Implementation

CHRISTABEL E. DADZIE, MAWUKO FUMEY, AND SULEIMAN NAMARA

WORLD BANK GROUP

Contents

Foreword

Projections for Africa indicate that the proportion of its youth population will be larger by 2035, which presents both opportunities and challenges. In Ghana, youth make up 36 percent of the population, and 56 percent of these youth live in urban areas. As the proportion of youth continues to grow, opportunities are emerging for harnessing this demographic dividend to boost socioeconomic growth in Ghana. To adequately respond, the government of Ghana will need to provide an enabling environment that facilitates the creation of decent job opportunities for new entrants to the labor market. Studies indicate that most jobs in Ghana are low-skill, requiring limited cognitive skills and technological content. This in turn translates into low earnings and less decent labor practices. The challenge for the government is therefore twofold: provide access to jobs and ensure that jobs meet decent work standards.

Over the last two decades, the government of Ghana has rolled out several interventions to address youth unemployment and underemployment. The current guiding policy, the Coordinated Programme of Economic and Social Development Policies (2017–24): An Agenda for Jobs—Creating Prosperity and Equal Opportunity for All, places the issues of youth unemployment and underemployment at the center of national development. Specific to programming, the revamping of the Youth Employment Agency (YEA), the work of the Microfinance and Small Loans Centre (MASLOC), and the operationalization of the Nation Builders Corps (NABCO) are avenues for promoting youth employment. In addition, implementation of the One-District-One-Factory, One-Village-One-Dam program and other sectoral initiatives are intended to revive formerly well-to-do but now-distressed businesses, as well as promote the establishment of strategic new businesses.

The Ministry of Employment and Labour Relations (MELR), which has the mandate to coordinate the agenda for creating decent jobs, has established systems that would provide accurate and timely information on the labor market for decision-making. The ministry collaborates with other state and nonstate actors to ensure that there is a close link between employment and social protection policies so unemployed persons who lack skills receive opportunities to acquire them and secure sustainable jobs. Furthermore, plans are under way to accelerate the transition of the informal economy into formal ventures in which the sustainability of jobs and labor protection would be assured for a majority of the labor force.

Addressing youth unemployment and underemployment remains central to the efforts of the World Bank globally and specifically in Ghana. The World Bank's 2016–19 Ghana Country Partnership Framework (CPF) called for promoting sustainable and more inclusive economic growth, improving skills, and creating jobs, particularly for youth. It is expected that the new CPF, currently under preparation, will also center on job creation. The World Bank's 2019 Systematic Country Diagnostic considers better-quality jobs to be one of the four pathways for promoting shared prosperity in Ghana, and it argues that skills development is a key input for such opportunities. The Systematic Country Diagnostic also calls for a stronger partnership between the government and the private sector to raise labor productivity and to create better-quality jobs. To harness the potential of Africa's youth, the World Bank's Africa Human Capital Plan emphasizes interventions to enhance skills and employability; connect workers to jobs; create more and better employment; boost labor market participation, especially that of women; and leverage technology while ensuring inclusivity in its use.

This report is another milestone along the road toward addressing the issue of youth unemployment in Ghana. It presents specific options that may be considered by the government in the short to medium terms to enhance coordination of youth employment programs for effectiveness and sustainability. We therefore call on all actors and stakeholders to review and share their views on the report's research findings and recommendations to enable implementation of viable options in both the public and private sectors.

The Ministry of Employment and Labour Relations and the World Bank will continue to work together toward enhanced human capital and promoting youth employment in Ghana.

Hon. Ignatius Baffour-Awuah, MP
Minister
Ministry of Employment and Labour Relations

Pierre Laporte
Country Director, Ghana
The World Bank

Acknowledgments

The authors of this study acknowledge the contributions from research conducted by Alex Ariho, youth employment consultant; Mpumelelo Nxumalo, social protection and jobs consultant; and Oyindamola Okuwa, research analyst. Appreciation also goes to Kathleen Beegle, former program leader; Johanne Buba, peer reviewer; Antonio Guiffrida, program leader, Human Development; Dhushyanth Raju, lead economist; Jamele Rigolini, peer reviewer; and Iffath Sharif, practice manager, Social Protection and Jobs, for the guidance provided to complete this study.

The study stems from both research and a series of stakeholder consultative workshops held between 2016 and 2018 and organized by the World Bank in partnership with Ghana's Ministry of Employment and Labour Relations. The authors are grateful to the Honorable Minister Ignatius Baffour-Awuah; the Honorable Deputy Minister Bright Wireko-Brobby; Emma Ofori-Agyeman, director for policy, planning, monitoring, and evaluation (PPME); and Ernest Berko, deputy director for PPME, for their leadership, commitment, and valuable contributions in promoting the youth employment agenda in Ghana and supporting the completion of this report.

The authors also express their sincere gratitude to the representatives of the ministries, agencies, departments, programs, nongovernmental organizations, civil society organizations, private sector actors, and youth networks that participated in the stakeholder consultative meetings and provided data and lessons on their programs.

The authors wish to thank as well all those who in diverse ways contributed to the compilation of this report.

Finally, the authors wish to recognize the generous grant from the World Bank's Rapid Social Response Trust Fund Program, without which this publication would not have been possible. The program is supported by Australia, Denmark, Norway, the Russian Federation, Sweden, the United Kingdom, and the Bill & Melinda Gates Foundation.

RAPID SOCIAL RESPONSE

About the Authors

Christabel E. Dadzie is a social protection specialist at the World Bank, based in Ghana. She is co-task team leader of the Ghana Productive Safety Net project and a core team member of the Ghana Jobs and Skills Project, which is currently being designed. She has also supported the World Bank's Liberia and Sierra Leone social protection teams. Before working at the World Bank, she worked on U.S. Agency for International Development projects, leading performance evaluations and program assessments, and she has worked within the United Nations system as a gender specialist. She has a master's degree in international affairs from Columbia University in New York.

Mawuko Fumey is a consultant with the Ghana Social Protection and Jobs team, providing support to lending operations and analytical work in Ghana. Equipped with almost two decades of experience in international development and with expertise covering capacity development, research and policy development, project management, and environmental management, she has led projects in various social sectors in Ghana. She has been certified as an organization and systems development consultant by the Gestalt Institute of Cleveland and has facilitated organizational learning and change management processes and stakeholder dialogues in Ghana.

Suleiman Namara is a senior social protection economist on the World Bank's South Asia Social Protection and Jobs team. He currently works as the program coordinator for the Rohingya Crisis Response in Dhaka. Suleiman has also led and supported investment lending operations, advisory services, and analytics, as well as policy dialogues. He has initiated and been involved in scaling up innovative systems-based safety nets and jobs programs in Africa and South Asia, including in fragile states. He was the task team leader for the Ghana Social Opportunities Project.

Executive Summary

Unemployment and underemployment are global development challenges. The World Bank's *World Development Report 2013,* on jobs, estimated that about 200 million youth are unemployed worldwide, so 600 million jobs will be needed over 15 years to maintain global employment rates (World Bank 2012). In Africa, projections indicate a youth bulge by 2035, presenting both opportunities and challenges. Currently, half of the region's population is under 25 years of age, and between 2015 and 2035 each year is expected to add a half-million more 15-year-olds. In Sub-Saharan Africa, because primary commodities still account for the bulk of exports, the volume of labor-intensive manufactured exports is limited. Nonwage work therefore remains prevalent, so the main challenge for employment creation is to increase the productivity of the informal sector.

The situation in Ghana is no different. In 2016 it was projected that, because of the country's growing youth population, 300,000 new jobs would have to be created each year to absorb the increasing number of unemployed young people. Yet the structure of the Ghanaian economy in terms of employment has not changed much from several decades ago. Most jobs are low-skilled, requiring limited cognitive or technology know-how. The quality of these jobs is reflected in low earnings and less decent work.[1] Thus an additional challenge for Ghana is creating access to an adequate number of high-quality, productive jobs.

This study seeks to increase knowledge about Ghana's job landscape and youth employment programs. The information can help policy makers and stakeholders identify ways to improve the programming and effectiveness of youth employment programs and strengthen coordination among major stakeholders. Although this study is not a policy document, it does provide a framework for short- to medium-term programming options for different groups of youths. The proposals are largely based on stakeholder consultations aimed at tapping into the experience and knowledge of key groups in this sector to produce ideas that reflect the realities on the ground and that ultimately will work (see appendix A). The proposals are also guided by national, regional, and global studies of youth employment policies and programs in Ghana and elsewhere (see appendixes B and C).

Any effort to address Ghana's youth unemployment and underemployment challenge must rely on focused strategic short-, medium-, and long-term responses. Although Ghana has launched a number of initiatives in response to this challenge, the lack of coordination among stakeholders in the sector has led to duplication. Key stakeholders on youth employment, including those in the private sector, currently have limited interaction. Regular exchanges are important for promoting synergies and reducing duplication of programs, and for sharing knowledge. Furthermore, Ghana lacks a comprehensive database on the characteristics of various categories of youth information—a database that is essential for the design and implementation of effective programs.

Without transformation of the current Ghanaian economic structure, employment opportunities will remain limited. A review is also needed of the country's education and training systems so they can equip young people with the requisite cognitive and soft skills and ethical values needed to thrive in today's workplace. Furthermore, the prevalent negative perception of technical and vocational education and training programs needs to change, so that people can appreciate the benefits that such programs offer both individuals and society as a whole.

As for the private sector, the government should seek to increase its participation in youth skills development and employment programs because its involvement has been shown to be critical to the success of such programs. The government could work with employers through public-private partnership (PPP) models to improve national systems for workforce development, including the curricula for training providers and national qualification frameworks for skills certification. Private sector employers could also offer apprenticeship and training programs tailored to market needs.

In Ghana, young women are limited in employment and entrepreneurial opportunities because of many economic and sociocultural factors, including lack of property rights, lack of access to capital, stereotypes, and limitations in the use of digital technology. Persons with disabilities are also mostly excluded from youth employment programs because of employer discrimination, a lack of disability-friendly facilities in the workplace, and a general view that they are "alms seekers" rather than productive members of society. This group also faces challenges in job search efforts.

Most existing government-led youth employment programs lack adequate systems for monitoring and evaluation and for impact measurement. Few programs include clear indicators that measure performance, and most do not carry out tracer studies to assess their effectiveness and what happens to beneficiaries once they have exited the programs. Without such systems and data, policy makers and other stakeholders find it difficult to make informed decisions on whether to fund or scale up a program or make changes for improvement.

Ghana's young people are a heterogeneous group. This study, then, offers youth training and employment strategies based on six categories of youth: (1) uneducated youth in rural areas; (2) uneducated youth in urban areas; (3) educated youth (secondary) in rural areas; (4) educated youth (secondary) in urban areas; (5) educated youth (tertiary) in rural areas; and (6) educated youth in urban areas. The study also proposes five priority areas based on stakeholder consultations and regional and global lessons. These are (1) promoting agriculture and agribusiness; (2) apprenticeship (skills training); (3) promoting entrepreneurship; (4) other high-yielding areas (renewable energy such as solar, construction, sports, and green jobs; and (5) preemployment support services.[2] Cross-cutting areas of attention reviewed include harnessing research and technology; promoting gender mainstreaming within programs; ensuring decent work for all, including the vulnerable; ensuring that some programs are private sector–driven; and effectively coordinating programming.

Finally, because of the fast-changing nature of work due to technology and artificial intelligence, today's labor market is rewarding different skills. Employers are putting a greater emphasis on cognitive and sociobehavioral skills such as critical thinking, emotional intelligence, teamwork, effective communication, and people management. Workers with these skills tend to be more adaptable to fast-changing labor markets. Technology is also changing how people work, giving rise to a free market economy in which organizations contract with independent workers for short-term engagements. Ghana therefore needs to develop an education and training system that is versatile and supports its young people in their efforts to adapt and thrive in the 21st-century world of work.

NOTES

1. The International Labour Organization (ILO) defines *decent work* as productive work for women and men under conditions of freedom, equality, security, and human dignity. It involves opportunities for work that delivers a fair income, provides security in the workplace, and ensures social protection for workers and their families.
2. "High-yielding areas" refer to areas of employment that provide the potential for high job creation.

REFERENCE

World Bank. 2012. *World Development Report 2013: Jobs.* Washington, DC: World Bank. http://documents.worldbank.org/curated/en/263351468330025810/World-development-report-2013-jobs.

Abbreviations

AGRA	Alliance for a Green Revolution in Africa
COTVET	Council for Technical and Vocational Education and Training
DANIDA	Denmark Development Cooperation
GCEEI	Ghana Centre for Entrepreneurship Employment and Innovation
GSTDP	Ghana Skills and Technology Development Project
ICT	information and communications technology
MELR	Ministry of Employment and Labour Relations
SMEs	small and medium enterprises
TVET	technical and vocational education and training

1 Introduction

OVERVIEW OF THE CURRENT YOUTH EMPLOYMENT LANDSCAPE

Over the years, the government of Ghana and private sector actors have introduced many policy interventions to address the country's high youth unemployment. An inventory carried out by the World Bank in 2016 listed 40 main youth employment programs, including 18 led by the public sector and 22 by the private sector. However, these programs appear to have had little impact because youth unemployment persists. And the challenge to Ghana will only take on added urgency as the number of new labor market entrants increases and outweighs job creation and as technology changes the nature of the job opportunities available for young people.

The *2015 Labour Force Report* (Ghana Statistical Service 2016) estimated that the overall unemployment rate in Ghana was 11.9 percent and that 12.1 percent of youth were unemployed. Meanwhile, disparities are found in the rural and urban employment rates. For example, the proportion of unemployed youth in urban areas (13.6 percent) is higher than that in rural areas (10.4 percent). Student enrollment rates vary based on level of education and drop sharply for secondary and higher education programs. The *Education Sector Performance Report 2016* estimates the transition rate from junior high school to senior high school to be 67 percent, whereas the completion rate for senior high school is projected to be 46 percent. Total high school enrollment for 2014/15 was estimated at 804,974 students, and enrollment at the tertiary level for the same school year totaled 320,746 students.

In 2016 Honorati and Johansson de Silva (2016) estimated that 300,000 jobs would have to be created annually from 2016 until 2020 to absorb the increasing number of youth workers. However, the employment structure of the Ghanaian economy has not seen much change over the last few decades. Most jobs in Ghana are low-skilled, requiring limited cognitive skills and technological know-how, and they generate low earnings. The main challenge for Ghana, then, is to create an adequate number of high-quality, productive jobs that could be filled by the youth emerging from employment and training programs.

Although the government has made a concerted effort to respond to this challenge, lack of coordination in the public sector has led to fragmentation of programs and duplication of effort. Changes in political preferences tend to disrupt the targeting, goals, and objectives of programs. The Ministry of Employment and Labour Relations (MELR) is the lead and coordinating ministry for employment issues at the programmatic level, but it has limited resources to effectively implement its mandate. Key functions of the ministry that should be strengthened include human resource planning, program monitoring and evaluation systems, and a comprehensive labor market information system, including management of public employment centers (PECs). The government should also establish a database on youth that takes into account their different backgrounds and needs. Such information is critical for designing and implementing effective youth employment programs.

Gaps in Ghana's youth employment programs, as identified through stakeholder consultations, include monitoring and evaluation, impact measurement, information systems, and the capacity to scale up. Most programs do not have clear indicators that measure performance, and monitoring and evaluation of existing programs are inadequate to ensure value for money. Furthermore, most programs do not have management information systems to boost monitoring and project management or to track efficiency. The major gaps in monitoring and evaluation make it challenging to identify ways to make funding decisions or scale up projects. Currently, the exit strategies for the beneficiaries of most national programs are not clear, nor are the returns on investment for most government programs.

OBJECTIVES OF THIS STUDY

This study seeks to maximize synergies and coalesce efforts around a shared approach toward job creation for Ghanaian youth. This approach would consist of pursuing the following strategies:

- Enhance the knowledge available to key stakeholders (researchers, policy makers, practitioners, and the private sector) about the landscape of youth employment programs in Ghana (see appendix A).
- Engage practitioners to identify real-life challenges and solutions to the youth unemployment phenomenon.
- Suggest a coherent approach to program planning and implementation.
- Propose systems for effective and sustainable service delivery, such as effective monitoring and evaluation and the use of management information systems to assist the government in its short- to medium-term planning.
- Identify concrete areas for promoting youth employment in Ghana based on global practices (see appendix B) and local best practices that offer opportunities for funding opportunities, effective implementation, and scaling up programs.

The objective of this study is to help the government of Ghana and other key stakeholders in the employment sector gain a clearer understanding of the current landscape of youth employment programs. Stakeholders can then use this knowledge to improve programming and coordination and to strengthen the effectiveness of these programs. This study provides options for short- to medium-term programming. These suggested options are guided by consultations with sector experts in Ghana, as well as regional and global studies and lessons in youth employment policies and programs.

This report has been prepared primarily based on data gathered through a series of stakeholder consultations with practitioners working in the field of youth employment in Ghana and with program beneficiaries, including youth networks and organizations (see appendix C). Research findings from national, regional, and global studies have also informed the report.

In addition to the rich qualitative information gathered through key stakeholder consultations, the report relies on the available national data, primarily from periodic surveys and reports prepared by the government, most of which are not very current. A lack of recent data is the main limitation of this report.

REFERENCES

Ghana Ministry of Education. 2016. *Education Sector Performance Report 2016*. Accra: Ghana Ministry of Education.

Ghana Statistical Service. 2016. *2015 Labour Force Report*. Accra: Ghana Statistical Service.

Honorati, Maddalena, and Sara Johansson de Silva. 2016. *Expanding Job Opportunities in Ghana*. Washington, DC: World Bank.

2 Background

GLOBAL AND COUNTRY CONTEXT

Unemployment and underemployment are a global development challenge. Development in any country is enhanced when productive jobs are created. With about 200 million youth unemployed worldwide, it is estimated that 600 million jobs will be needed over 15 years to maintain the current global employment rates (World Bank 2012). Globally, the private sector tends to create the majority of jobs, whereas in most developing countries the majority of jobs are in the informal sector. It is thus critical to increase labor and sector productivity to create more decent jobs, especially in agrarian countries.[1]

In Africa, projections indicate a youth bulge by 2035, which presents opportunities as well as challenges for countries. Currently, half of Africa's population is under 25 years of age, and it is projected that between 2015 and 2035 each year will see an increase of a half-million more 15-year-olds than the year before (Filmer and Fox 2014). In Sub-Saharan Africa, primary commodities still account for the bulk of exports, whereas the volume of labor-intensive manufactured exports is limited. Nonwage work accounts for more than 80 percent of women's employment. The main challenge for employment creation is increasing the productivity of the informal sector, which employs nearly four-fifths of the region's workforce (Filmer and Fox 2014).

The situation in Ghana is no different. Until recently, the country's economy had been on a high growth path, mainly attributable to the sharp increase in the prices of its main commodity exports, cocoa and gold, and the launch of commercial oil and natural gas production in 2011. This boom has allowed the country to make significant progress in reducing poverty over the past decade. Ghana met the Millennium Development Goal (MDG) of halving poverty ahead of the target period, with the share of the population living in poverty falling from 52 percent in 1991 to 24 percent in 2012 (Ghana Statistical Service 2014; Molini and Paci 2015). Meanwhile, the country saw significant improvements in health, education, and other areas important for individual and social well-being.

Between 2005 and 2012, Ghana created a considerable number of jobs while increasing total labor productivity. Job creation averaged 3.2 percent a year between 1991 and 2005 and rose to 4 percent a year on average between 2005 and 2012—a time when annual growth of gross domestic product (GDP) averaged 8 percent. Labor force participation for 15- to 64-year-olds remained high (at 80 percent of the total population), even as the share of youth (15- to 24-year-olds) enrolled in school increased from 21 percent to 31 percent and unemployment rates fell from 4 percent to 2 percent between 2005 and 2012. Furthermore, labor productivity increased from 1991 to 2005 following a boom in the service sectors (mostly in financial, communications, and storage services). It rose even higher from 2005 to 2012, driven by the rapid expansion of the extractive and construction sectors (Honorati and Johansson de Silva 2016).

Growth and job creation were accompanied by rapid urbanization and a gradual structural transformation of Ghana's economy, as agricultural work largely gave way to jobs in services and, to a lesser degree, to industrial jobs.

As the economy underwent this sectoral transformation, employment also shifted toward self-employment off the farm (especially in urban areas) and, to a lesser extent, to private wage employment. Over the last two decades, the share of off-farm self-employment as a share of total employment increased from 26 percent to 36 percent. Over the same period, private wage employment nearly tripled, from 6 percent to 16 percent, while the share of public wage work fell from 9 percent to 6 percent. In the last decade, half (1.5 million) of new jobs have been created in the off-farm self-employment sector and in urban areas, especially the Greater Accra and Ashanti regions (Honorati and Johansson de Silva 2016).

Ghana is currently facing major challenges in diversifying and sustaining its economic growth because its growth model has depended on natural resources, especially with the launch of commercial oil production. Also, the manufacturing sector, which otherwise should create jobs, has stagnated, while most of the new jobs have been created in low-wage, low-productivity trade services.

YOUTH EMPLOYMENT AND UNEMPLOYMENT TRENDS IN GHANA

According to Ghana's *2015 Labour Force Report,* the overall unemployment rate in Ghana is an estimated 11.9 percent (Ghana Statistical Service 2016). Persons with a secondary school education have the highest rate of unemployment (24.4 percent), while those with a postsecondary education or more have recorded the lowest rate (13 percent). With respect to youth, it is estimated that 59.6 percent are employed, 12.1 percent are unemployed, and the rest are not in the labor force (Ghana Statistical Service 2016).[2] More males (62.8 percent) than females (57.2 percent) are employed, and the majority (90 percent) of employed youth are engaged by the private sector. The proportion of unemployed youth is higher in urban (13.6 percent) than in rural (10.4 percent) areas. The civil and public services together employ 8.4 percent of youth. The labor force participation rate of youth is 71.7 percent, and it is higher among males (75.1 percent) than females (69.2 percent) and higher in rural areas than in urban areas.[3] The employment status of youth is presented in figure 2.1.

In terms of the number of hours worked per week, only 18.5 percent of employed youth work between 30 and 39 hours per week, whereas 45.5 percent work less than 30 hours per week. The rest (17.5 percent) work more than 49 hours per week. More than one-fifth of employed youth (22.4 percent) work 20–29 hours per week.

FIGURE 2.1
Employment status of youth population, Ghana

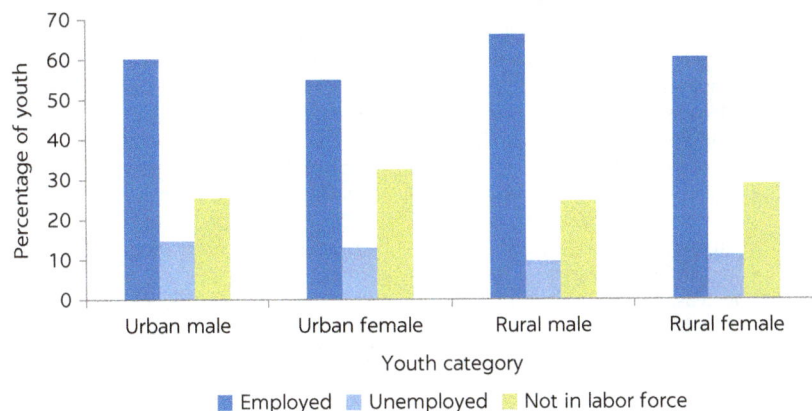

Source: Compiled from Ghana Statistical Service (2016).

SITUATION ANALYSIS: DEMAND- AND SUPPLY-SIDE CHALLENGES

As noted, Ghana has faced macroeconomic challenges, particularly related to its dependence on natural resources for economic growth, which also have contributed to stagnation of its manufacturing sector. Growth in manufacturing declined for a range of reasons, including rising interest rates, higher production and distribution costs, aging or obsolete equipment, inefficient infrastructure services, and low productivity. So far, neither the oil nor the manufacturing sector has produced as many jobs as expected. Under this growth model, most of the new jobs created have been in low-earning, low-productivity trade services, with 25 percent of the population working in this sector (Honorati and Johansson de Silva 2016).

Ghana is currently categorized as a high-potential, lower-middle-income country. Table 2.1 is an overview of the youth employment challenge, as well as the overall economic inclusive growth challenge of the country.

One of the factors contributing to the current unemployment challenge in Ghana is the lack of job opportunities in the formal sector.[4] Private sector formal employment accounts for about 2 percent of total employment, whereas informal firms and household enterprises account for 54 percent (Honorati and Johansson de Silva 2016). Alongside the challenges posed by the economic environment, the outcomes of interventions aimed at creating jobs in microenterprises and small and medium enterprises have been mixed. Many interventions have provided financial and technical support for household enterprises as a job creation strategy. However, research shows that these enterprises often tend to not grow and rarely employ additional workers; nor do they grow into large firms because of various constraints, including (1) lack of the technical and business knowledge needed to effectively manage their business and expand; (2) limited access to financing; and (3) limited access to large markets (Buba and Reyes 2019).

According to the World Bank's 2013 Enterprise Survey, in Ghana an inadequately educated labor force ranks higher as a constraint to hiring than

TABLE 2.1 **Overview: Ghana's inclusive growth and youth employment challenges**

COUNTRY DESCRIPTION	INCLUSIVE GROWTH CHALLENGE	YOUTH EMPLOYMENT CHALLENGE
High-potential, lower-middle-income country	• Quality of human capital is too low. • Higher secondary completion and job readiness rates are needed. • Management skills are scarce. • Transformation is tilted toward services. • Financial sector is underdeveloped with poorly managed infrastructure. • Urban governance is poor. • In Sub-Saharan Africa, a continuous increase in fertility leads to higher population.	• Investments in labor-intensive enterprises are insufficient to accelerate transformation and grow wage employment. • Secondary and higher education curricula require changes to better reflect labor market needs. • Commercial agriculture opportunities are inadequate for rural youth. • Challenges in land access and access to markets also prevail.

Source: Fox and Kaul 2017.

labor regulations.[5] Another major constraint identified during consultations with industry experts is the skills mismatch—that is, the skills of potential employees are mostly irrelevant to industry needs. The government of Ghana's medium-term development policy framework document, "An Agenda for Jobs: Creating Prosperity and Equal Opportunity for All," also identifies the skills mismatch as a key challenge for reducing unemployment (Ghana National Development Planning Commission 2017). The government intends to address this issue through its strategic plans for education and for technical and vocational education and training (TVET).

The country's educational system sends about 210,000 unemployable unskilled and semiskilled young Ghanaians (including about 60 percent of graduates at various education levels and those who exit early) into the labor market each year (Ghana Ministry of Employment and Labour Relations 2014). The quality of education in Ghana and the weak link between the education sector and the productive sectors of the economy remain major challenges. Academic training in Ghana is generally not aligned with labor market dynamics, which constantly call for new and different skill sets. In addition, the usage and application of technology are limited, but those tools are critical, given the changing nature of work. Preemployment support services are minimal, and most of the existing services are ineffective, particularly those offered by public training academic institutions. Over the years, this situation has resulted in a large pool of unemployed youth who are ill prepared for the job market.

Ghana's TVET sector needs major reforms as well. Service delivery in this sector is fragmented, and coordination among key stakeholders is minimal. Challenges confronting the sector include (1) poor links between training institutions and industry; (2) a deeply fragmented landscape and lack of coordination among TVET delivery agencies; (3) a multiplicity of standards, testing, and certification systems; (4) low-quality instruction due to inadequate instructor training and lack of instructional support and infrastructure; (5) an informal TVET system that has been neglected and detached from the formal sector; and (6) poor public perceptions of technical and vocational programs, which are viewed as a track for academically weak students (Ghana Ministry of Education 2018). The government has produced a strategic plan for the transformation of the sector (2018–22) to guide the implementation of TVET reforms.

CONSTRAINTS FACED BY YOUTH

Youth make up about 36 percent of Ghana's population. Of these, about 54 percent live in urban areas (Ghana Statistical Service 2018). More females (56.2 percent) live in urban areas than males (54.9 percent). To effectively address the needs of youth, the government has classified them in seven categories: (1) male and female; (2) rural and urban; (3) adolescence and adult; (4) physically challenged and able-bodied; (5) educated and uneducated; (6) skilled and unskilled; and (7) in school and out of school (Ghana Ministry of Youth and Sports 2010).

The *2015 Labour Force Report* estimates that 40 percent of Ghanaian youth have no education, and only 3.8 percent have acquired a tertiary education qualification (Ghana Statistical Service 2016). Education empowers people to live healthier lives and attain more productive livelihoods and can break the poverty cycle. The level of education attained can also influence people's aspirations in life. Figure 2.2 provides a breakdown of the education levels of Ghanaian youth.

The 2015 Ghana labor force survey estimates that more males (5.4 percent) have a tertiary-level education than females (2.6 percent), and more than half (57.0 percent) of youth living in rural areas have no education compared with 26.3 percent of their urban counterparts (Ghana Statistical Service 2016). Only 1.7 percent of youth in rural areas have a tertiary education compared with 5.6 percent of their urban counterparts (see figures 2.3 and 2.4).

Until recently, education in public schools in Ghana had been compulsory and free through junior high school. In September 2017, the Ghanaian government expanded this policy to the senior high school level. The country has seen gains in enrollment over the years, but transition rates from the junior secondary level to the senior secondary level and from the senior secondary level to the tertiary level still require some attention. The transition rate from junior high to senior high school is 67 percent, and the completion rate is 46 percent. Total enrollment for 2014/15 at the senior high school level is estimated to have been

FIGURE 2.2

Education status of youth population, Ghana

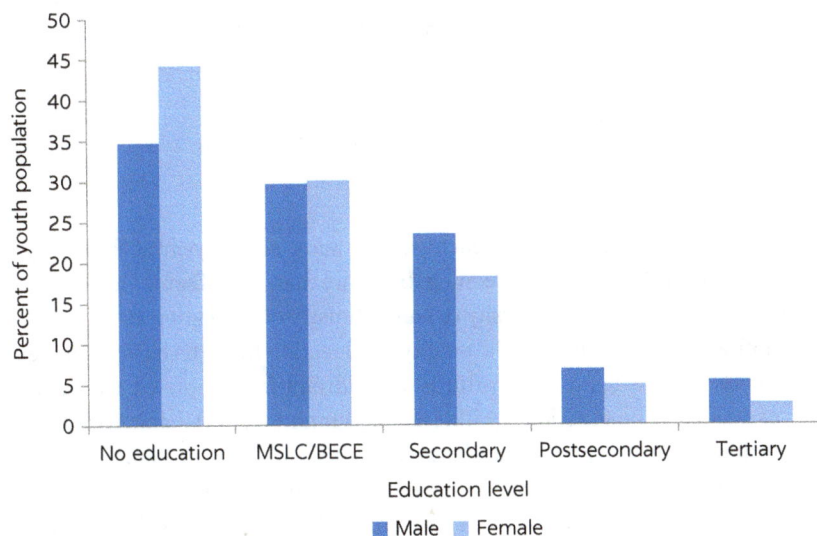

Source: Compiled from Ghana Statistical Service (2016).
Note: BECE = Basic Education Certificate Examination; MSLC = Middle School Leaving Certificate.

FIGURE 2.3

Education status of youth population in urban areas, Ghana

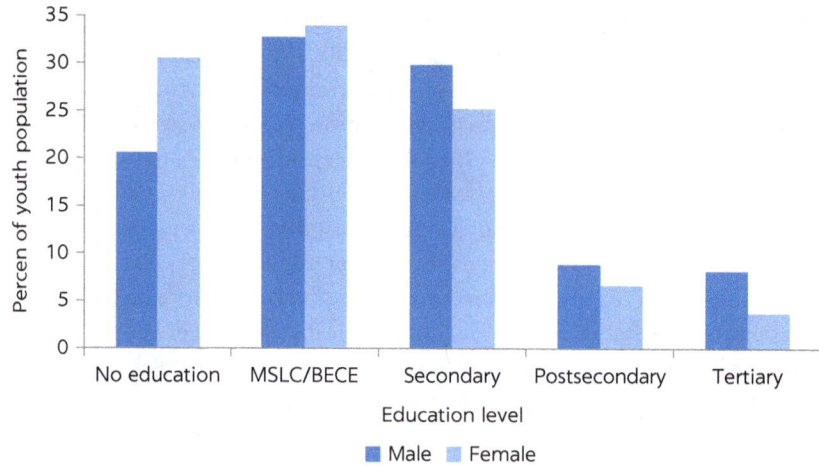

Source: Compiled from Ghana Statistical Service (2016).
Note: BECE = Basic Education Certificate Examination; MSLC = Middle School Leaving Certificate.

FIGURE 2.4

Education status of youth population in rural areas, Ghana

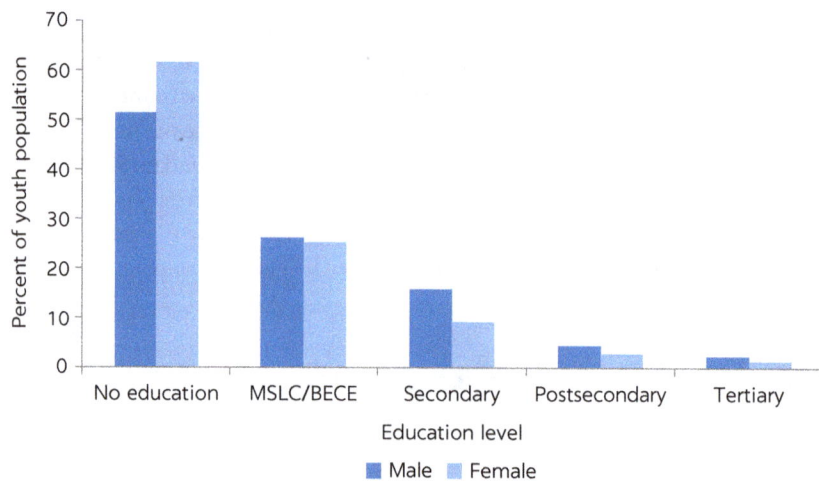

Source: Compiled from Ghana Statistical Service (2016).
Note: BECE = Basic Education Certificate Examination; MSLC = Middle School Leaving Certificate.

804,974 students, whereas enrollment for the same school year at the tertiary level totaled 320,746 students, meaning that more than half of senior high school graduates did not go to a university (Ghana Ministry of Education 2016).

Another challenge involves the quality of education from the basic to the tertiary levels, with as many as two-thirds of children who complete basic education estimated to be functionally illiterate and innumerate (Ghana Ministry of Education 2013). At the tertiary level, the major issue is the employability of students, as expressed during the stakeholder consultations. Many graduates of vocational and technical schools and universities lack the skills desired by employers, such as analytical and critical reasoning, communications skills, information and communications technology (ICT) competencies, a strong work ethic, and entrepreneurship.

Youth who choose to venture into entrepreneurship face additional constraints. These include the current weak support systems for entrepreneurship and small-scale business development for self-employment (Ghana Ministry of Employment and Labour Relations 2014). Stakeholder consultations confirm limitations in accessing physical resources such as land, equipment, and financial capital, especially by youth. Other challenges encountered by youth (similar to the challenges faced by those starting businesses) include lack of technology, high transport costs, an unattractive business environment, lack of relevant experience, lack of and inaccessible skilled labor, high registration costs, high costs to obtain licenses to operate formally, and lack of networking opportunities.

The broader environment can influence how young people develop aspirations and work toward realizing these aspirations. A study by the Youth Forward Initiative in 2018 of the aspirations of young people in Ghana and their thoughts about work reveals differences in the aspirations of young people in rural and urban settings. Poverty influences young people's hopes.[6] Young people in rural areas have limited role models and experiences from which to develop aspirations compared with their urban counterparts, who are exposed to a much wider range of professions and options, including the social message that "office work" is more respectable. Instead of considering longer-term goals, most young people in rural areas prefer work with a daily income, instead of weekly or monthly wages, to meet their short-term survival needs.

As in other parts of the world, the rapidly changing requirements of the world of work due to technology disruptions are likely to affect the job readiness of Ghanaian youth. It is estimated that globally, the number of jobs requiring digital skills will grow by 12 percent by 2024 (Robinson et al. 2018). As more firms adopt technology, automation is likely to increase, creating temporary displacements. The McKinsey Global Institute estimates that by 2030 half of all current work activities could be automated, and that in roughly 60 percent of jobs at least one-third of duties could be automated. These projections will mean significant changes for workers and workplaces, and competition for low-skilled jobs may increase for those who do not have the expertise to compete for higher-skilled ones. Employers are already focusing on new skill sets and core competencies—such as teamwork, problem solving, communication, and analytical skills—and they have made these key selection criteria for job applicants. A critical step would be to assess the readiness of the Ghanaian youth population to take advantage of this new reality and the rise of the gig economy (Bughin et al. 2018).[7]

Stakeholder consultations revealed that elements of preemployment support services exist across the country in the form of internships and guidance and counseling units in schools. However, Ghana lacks a structured policy guiding internships and work-based learning (WBL) that would result in a systematic approach to implementing preemployment support services.[8] Most youth lack the right work ethic and attitudes that would enable them to secure jobs and to sustain their employability. Existing programs often do not offer basic services, such as guidance on how to write résumés and application letters and how to sit for a job interview. The country also has few online job platforms offering job search and placement assistance. Soft skills training on values and work attitudes should be integrated into the regular curricula of educational institutions. It should contribute toward preparing youth to transition smoothly from school to work and make available to them resources that will boost their employability and sustain them in productive jobs.

NOTES

1. The International Labour Organization (ILO) defines *decent work* as productive work for women and men under conditions of freedom, equality, security, and human dignity. It involves opportunities for work that delivers a fair income, provides security in the workplace, and ensures social protection for workers and their families.
2. The youth unemployment rate measures the percentage of employable youth in a country's workforce—that is, the population 15–35 years of age who during the reference period were without jobs and were seeking a job or were available for work.
3. The labor force participation rate is the percentage of the working-age population that is either employed or unemployed.
4. Formal sector employees are usually those with recognized income sources for paying income taxes based on 40-hour, regular wage jobs.
5. World Bank, Enterprise Survey 2013: Ghana 2012–14, https://microdata.worldbank.org /index.php/catalog/2181.
6. The Youth Forward Initiative is part of a Mastercard Foundation youth employment program with funding of US$74 million in Ghana and Uganda. The Youth Forward Initiative brings together multiple organizations to train and help transition 200,000 young people into sustainable jobs in the construction and agriculture sectors.
7. The gig economy is made up of three main components: (1) independent workers paid by the gig (a task or a project), as opposed to those workers who receive a salary or hourly wage; (2) consumers who need a specific service, such as a ride to their next destination or a particular item delivered; and (3) companies that connect the worker to the consumer in a direct manner, including app-based technology platforms (https://www.naco.org /featured-resources/future-work-rise-gig-economy).
8. Work-based learning is an educational strategy that provides students with real-life work experiences to which they can apply academic and technical skills and develop their employability.

REFERENCES

Buba, Johanne, and Aterido Reyes. 2019. "Firm Level Interventions for Jobs." World Bank, Washington, DC.

Bughin, Jacques, Eric Hazen, Susan Lund, Peter Dahlström, Anna Wiesinger, and Amresh Subramanian. 2018. "Skill Shift Automation and the Future of the Workforce." Discussion paper, McKinsey Global Institute, Brussels.

Filmer, Deon, and Louise Fox. 2014. *Youth Employment in Sub-Saharan Africa*. Africa Development Series. Washington, DC: World Bank.

Fox, Louise, and Upaasna Kaul. 2017. "The Evidence Is In: How Should Youth Employment Programs in Low-Income Countries Be Designed?" U.S. Agency for International Development, Washington, DC.

Ghana Ministry of Education. 2013. *Education Sector Performance Report 2013*. Accra: Ghana Ministry of Education.

Ghana Ministry of Education. 2016. *Education Sector Performance Report 2016*. Accra: Ghana Ministry of Education.

Ghana Ministry of Education. 2018. "Strategic Plan for TVET Transformation, 2018–2022." Council for Technical and Vocational Education and Training, Accra.

Ghana Ministry of Employment and Labour Relations. 2014. "National Employment Policy." Accra. http://www.melr.gov.gh/wp-content/uploads/2015/12/National-Employment -Policy-2015.pdf.

Ghana Ministry of Youth and Sports. 2010. "National Youth Policy of Ghana." Accra.

Ghana National Development Planning Commission. 2017. "An Agenda for Jobs: Creating Prosperity and Equal Opportunity for All." https://s3-us-west-2.amazonaws.com/new -ndpc-static1/CACHES/PUBLICATIONS/2018/08/23/Medium-term+Policy +Framework-Final+June+2018.pdf.

Ghana Statistical Service. 2014. "Poverty Profile in Ghana (2005–2013)." Accra.

Ghana Statistical Service. 2016. *2015 Labour Force Report*. Accra: Ghana Statistical Service.

Ghana Statistical Service. 2018. "Ghana Living Standards Survey Round 7 (GLSS 7). Poverty Trends in Ghana 2005–2017." Accra.

Honorati, Maddalena, and Sara Johansson de Silva. 2016. *Expanding Job Opportunities in Ghana*. Washington, DC: World Bank.

Molini, V., and P. Paci. 2015. "Poverty Reduction in Ghana: Progress and Challenges." World Bank, Washington, DC.

Robinson, Danielle Simone, Namita Datta, Emily Massey, Tshegofatso Kgasago, Mishkah Jakoet, Peter J. Glick, Diana Gehlhaus Carew, et al. 2018. *Digital Jobs for Youth: Young Women in the Digital Economy. Solutions for Youth Employment*. Washington, DC: World Bank Group, Solutions for Youth Employment (S4YE). http://documents.worldbank.org/curated/en/503651536154914951/Digital-Jobs-for-Youth-Young-Women-in-the-Digital-Economy.

World Bank. 2012. *World Development Report 2013: Jobs*. Washington, DC: World Bank. http://documents.worldbank.org/curated/en/263351468330025810/World-development-report-2013-jobs.

World Bank. 2014. *Youth Employment in Sub-Saharan Africa*. Washington, DC: World Bank.

3 Policies Guiding Youth Employment

GLOBAL CONTEXT

Ghana subscribes to international policies that guide youth employment. What follows is an overview of some of these policies.

In 1995 the United Nations General Assembly adopted the World Programme of Action for Youth, which originally covered 10 priority areas and proposals for action. After a decade of implementation, member states added five more youth priority areas, which were adopted as a supplement in 2007. These areas are expected to guide policy and action in youth development. Four proposals address employment, specifying actions that governments are encouraged to embrace: (1) creating opportunities for self-employment; (2) generating employment for specific groups of young people (such as women, persons with disabilities, youth returning from military service, migrant youth, refugee youth, displaced persons, street children, and indigenous youth); (3) offering free services to support young people trying to gain knowledge and experience in preparation for permanent work; and (4) creating opportunities in fields that are rapidly evolving as a result of technological innovation.

In 2012 the International Labour Organization (ILO), during its International Labor Conference, adopted a Call for Action on Youth Employment as an immediate response to the youth employment challenge. In its 2030 Agenda for Sustainable Development, the United Nations (UN) emphasizes in Goal 8 youth employment. The goal calls for promoting inclusive and sustainable economic growth, employment, and decent work for all. In 2015 the United Nations' Chief Executives Board approved the Global Initiative on Decent Jobs for Youth to scale up action in support of youth employment. This first-ever UN systemwide initiative is intended to help UN member states implement the Sustainable Development Goals (SDGs), specifically SDG 8, and it serves as a blueprint for broad collaboration and partnership among all key actors, including social partners, youth organizations, and the public and private sectors.[1] It is guided by a series of principles, such as respect for human rights and the application of international labor standards, the promotion of gender equality, and a multidimensional and multisectoral approach. This framework enjoins the global development community to develop and operationalize a global strategy for youth employment and also to implement by 2030 the Global Jobs Pact of the International Labour Organization.

The Global Initiative on Decent Jobs for Youth has four strategies: (1) create a strategic multistakeholder alliance; (2) expand and scale up regional and country-level action on decent jobs for youth; (3) establish a knowledge facility on decent jobs for youth; and (4) set up funding modalities and resource mobilization.[2]

At the regional level, in May 2016 the African Development Bank (AfDB) launched the Jobs for Youth in Africa (JfYA) Strategy for 2016–25, with the aim of creating 25 million jobs and equipping 50 million African youth with professional, transferable, and soft skills in 10 years. The purpose of this initiative is to enhance the employability of young people and the success rate of young entrepreneurs. To achieve this goal, the AfDB launched the ENABLE Youth program, which is being implemented across a number of African countries, including Ghana.

COUNTRY CONTEXT

Ghana has introduced several policies to guide strategies and the implementation of interventions specific to youth employment issues. These include the National Youth Policy, National Employment Policy, National Social Protection Policy, and Labor-Intensive Public Works Policy. These policies all contribute to the common objective of promoting jobs and employment for youth, although overlaps in institutional mandates exist. This section describes the current policies and how they contribute to youth employment in Ghana.

With employment creation at the forefront of the government of Ghana's development agenda, authorities have launched several policy initiatives, both broad and specific, to address the unemployment challenge. Past national development frameworks—such as the National Medium-Term Development Plan (NMTDP), 2014–17, and the Ghana Shared Growth and Development Agenda (GSGDA I and II)—have made special provisions for youth employment and development to address the fact that a significant proportion of youth remain unemployed or employed in low-wage jobs

The government launched the National Youth Employment Programme (NYEP) in 2006 to provide skills training and jobs for youth as part of its efforts to tackle youth unemployment, underemployment, and food insecurity. In 2012, with a new government in power, the institution was restructured into the Ghana Youth Employment and Entrepreneurial Development Agency (GYEEDA), which was in turn restructured into the Youth Employment Agency (YEA) under Act 887 in 2015. The agency's objective is to provide skills training and apprenticeship modules to support youth during the transition from unemployment to employment. In 2016 Parliament passed the Youth Employment Agency Regulations, 2016 (L.I. 2231), for the effective implementation of the provisions of Act 887.

In 2010 the government launched the National Youth Policy to provide guidelines for all stakeholders involved in the implementation of policies, programs, and projects for the development of youth. This was followed by the National Youth Policy Implementation Plan, 2014–17. The policy has 19 priority areas, which are further categorized into four main areas: (1) human development and technology; (2) economic empowerment (youth and employment features within this area); (3) youth participation, governance, and leadership; and

(4) culture, sports, and national orientation. In the area of youth employment, the policy focuses on (1) building the capacity of youth to discover wealth-creating opportunities by providing them with access to reliable and adequate labor market information; (2) creating opportunities for young people to take advantage of available jobs; (3) training and preparing them for the global market; (4) and incorporating entrepreneurial skills into curricula (Ghana Ministry of Youth and Sports 2014). In 2016 Parliament passed the National Youth Authority Act (Act 939), which gave the National Youth Authority a mandate to formulate policies and implement programs that promote youth development and the effective participation of youth in the economic development of the country.

In 2014 the Ministry of Employment and Labour Relations (MELR) launched the National Employment Policy. This policy is aimed particularly at generating employment opportunities for vulnerable groups, youth, women, and the disabled. The goal of the policy is to create decent, gainful employment opportunities so workers in the country's growing labor force can improve their living conditions and contribute to economic growth and national development within the framework of equity, fairness, security, and dignity (Ghana Ministry of Employment and Labour Relations 2014).

The government launched the Ghana National Social Protection Policy in 2015 to address social inequalities and to provide economic opportunities for the extremely poor. The policy seeks to provide effective and efficient social assistance to reduce extreme poverty and to promote productive inclusion and decent work. It also seeks to substantially reduce the proportion of youth not in employment, education, or training (NEET) by 2020 and by 2030 to increase by 75 percent the number of youth and adults that possess skills relevant to employment, decent jobs, and entrepreneurship, including technical and vocational skills. It proposes as well to help the country achieve full and productive employment and decent work for all women and men, including young people and persons with disabilities (Ghana Ministry of Gender, Children, and Social Protection 2015).

In 2016 the government introduced the National Labour-Intensive Public Works Policy (LiPW) to improve the living conditions of the economically active poor through expansion of income-earning opportunities and accelerated local economic development. Labor-intensive public works are directed at enhancing job opportunities for the economically active poor, with the goal of transforming local economies and enhancing local employable skills and capacity development and promoting decent work standards.

In 2017 the new government administration developed "The Coordinated Programme of Economic and Social Development Policies (2017–2024): An Agenda for Jobs: Creating Prosperity and Equal Opportunity for All." It then followed up with a medium-term development framework, "An Agenda for Jobs: Creating Prosperity and Equal Opportunity for All (2018–2021)." These two frameworks define Ghana's strategic direction for job creation over the next five years. One objective is aimed at building human capital through improved access to high-quality education and health to create an employable and competitive labor force.

Table 3.1 is a summary of four policies on youth employment in Ghana presented around the following themes:

- Human development and technology
- Economic empowerment
- Youth participation, governance, and leadership
- Social protection and national orientation

TABLE 3.1 **Analysis of policies contributing to youth employment in Ghana**

OVERALL CATEGORY	NATIONAL YOUTH POLICY	NATIONAL EMPLOYMENT POLICY	NATIONAL SOCIAL PROTECTION POLICY	LABOR-INTENSIVE PUBLIC WORKS POLICY
Policy goal	Empower youth to contribute positively to national development	Create gainful and decent employment opportunities for the growing labor force to improve workers' living conditions and contribute to economic growth and national development within the framework of equity, fairness, security, and dignity	Deliver a well-coordinated, intersectoral social protection system enabling people to live in dignity through income support, livelihood empowerment, and improved access to systems of basic services	Improve the living conditions of the economically active poor through expansion of income-earning opportunities and accelerated local economic development
Human development and technology	Make development and delivery of education and skills training more responsive to the labor market; build the capacity of youth in science, research, and appropriate technology; and provide easy access to ICT infrastructure	Prepare a national human resource development plan that identifies present and future skills needs and related training programs; promote a national apprenticeship system that develops worker proficiency in relevant skill areas, industry, and craftspersonship; integrate career guidance and counseling into the school system	Achieve full and productive employment and decent work for all women and men, including for young people and persons with disabilities, by 2030	Provide employable vocational and technical skills for the unskilled and semiskilled labor forces; provide socioeconomic infrastructure for sustainable local economic development
Economic empowerment	Build capacity of youth to tap wealth-creating opportunities; enable access to reliable and adequate labor market information; mainstream entrepreneurship into school curricula; integrate entrepreneurial skills into youth development activities, facilitate access to credit, and celebrate young entrepreneurs as role models; promote participation of youth in modern agriculture as a viable career opportunity	Create more decent jobs to meet the demand for employment; promote investment in strategic sectors of the economy; promote incentives for business development, innovation, and employment of targeted groups, including young graduates and the vulnerable; prioritize TVET for job seekers planning to enter into self-employment	Promote productive inclusion and decent work to sustain families and communities at risk; by 2030 increase by 75 percent the number of youth and adults with the skills relevant to employment, decent jobs, and entrepreneurship, including technical and vocational skills; by 2020 substantially reduce the proportion of youth not in employment, education, or training	Create income-generating opportunities for the rural and urban poor to reduce extreme poverty; promote private sector participation in job creation and sustainable local economic development
Youth participation, governance, and leadership	Provide equitable conditions for both males and females; build synergies through networking and partnerships and create mentorship opportunities	Increase access to labor market information for all youth, especially in rural areas; provide special assistance for the development of female entrepreneurship		Ensure gender equity
Social protection and national orientation	Provide social protection for vulnerable and excluded youth; inculcate a spirit of nationalism, patriotism, and volunteerism among youth	Prioritize use of labor-intensive approaches in the production of public goods and services; enforce employment protection regulations; institute measures to ensure that people with disabilities and people living with HIV/AIDS are fully mainstreamed into the labor market	Achieve fully equal pay for work of equal value by 2030	Improve the welfare of the economically poor, the vulnerable, and the disadvantaged

Source: World Bank.
Note: ICT = information and communications technology; TVET = technical and vocational education and training.

INSTITUTIONS IMPLEMENTING YOUTH EMPLOYMENT POLICY

Agencies and institutions in different sectors oversee youth employment in Ghana. This section describes the main public sector institutions that have mandates to promote youth employment.

The Ministry of Employment and Labour Relations and its technical departments and agencies are responsible for the overall coordination and implementation of the National Employment Policy. The ministry is supported by the National Development Planning Commission (NDPC). In addition, under the National Employment Policy, it will be assisted by the National Employment Coordinating Council (NECC), which is expected to consist of representatives of employment-generating sectors, partners, and ministries overseeing resource mobilization, monitoring and evaluation, and job creation.[3] Currently, MELR chairs the Employment Sector Working Group, which brings together stakeholders in that sector to review progress and address the challenges in tackling Ghana's unemployment issues.

The National Youth Policy and the National Youth Authority Act 939 mandate the National Youth Authority (NYA) to formulate, implement, and coordinate programs that promote the well-being of youth. Other youth agencies, such as the Youth Employment Agency and the National Service Scheme (NSS), seek to facilitate the promotion of short-term youth employment opportunities and instill a sense of nationalism among youth.

The contributions of key institutions (ministries, agencies, and coordinating agencies) to job creation are presented in the following sections.

Ministries

- *Ministry of Employment and Labour Relations (MELR)*. In addition to its overarching role coordinating employment, MELR issues labor market information in collaboration with the Ghana Statistical Service and other labor organizations so that relevant up-to-date data are available for policy research, planning, and formulation. The ministry also has a leading role in creating an enabling environment for job creation.
- *Ministry of Youth and Sports (MoYS)*. The MoYS oversees youth development policies and their implementation.
- *Ministry of Education (MoE)*. The MoE has oversight responsibility for education sector policies and currently oversees all TVET policies and program implementation.
- *Ministry of Finance (MoF)*. The MoF ensures that budgets for ministries, departments, and agencies are adequate for formulating employment-centered growth strategies and include incentives that attract the private sector to invest in job creation.
- *Ministry of Local Government and Rural Development (MLGRD)*. The MLGRD facilitates the implementation of job and employment programs in line with existing local government structures. It also ensures that development activities and the investments of the municipality and metropolis district assemblies promote productive employment and income generation opportunities.
- *Ministry of Food and Agriculture (MoFA)*. The MoFA ensures that policies and programs encourage youth to seek employment in the agriculture and

agribusiness value chains. This ministry also designs programs that include incentives for the private sector to invest in large-scale agricultural initiatives that ultimately generate jobs.

- *Ministry of Gender, Children, and Social Protection (MoGCSP)*. The MoGCSP ensures that beneficiaries of social assistance programs who have productive capacity are linked with job training or job placement initiatives.
- *Ministry of Trade and Industry (MoTI)*. MoTI develops effective trade and industrial strategies for national development. This ministry also formulates policies that facilitate the development of enterprises, including micro, small, and medium enterprises.
- *Ministry of Business Development (MoBD)*. The MoBD was created in 2017 with a mandate to promote a favorable business environment and to support the activities of the private sector, including a focus on youth entrepreneurship.

Coordinating agencies

- *National Development Planning Commission (NDPC)*. The NDPC is responsible for national development planning and ensuring that the long-term development goal of the National Employment Policy is adequately integrated into the country's medium- and long-term development plans.
- *Ghana Statistical Service (GSS)*. The GSS provides labor statistics and undertakes periodic surveys of the country's labor force and employment situation in both the formal and informal sectors of the national economy.

Other public institutions

- *Microfinance and Small Loans Centre (MASLOC)*. MASLOC provides financial and nonfinancial assistance—such as credit, market information, and other business advisory and extension services—to micro, small, and medium enterprises.

Stakeholder groups

- *National Employment Coordinating Council (NECC)*. The NECC is expected to assist the Ministry of Employment and Labour Relations and its various departments and agencies in implementing the National Employment Policy.
- *Employment Sector Working Group*. This group comprises development partner representatives, private sector actors, and representatives of key implementing ministries. It promotes the Ministry of Employment and Labour Relations' coordinating role to engage ministries, departments, and agencies working on the jobs agenda.

Figure 3.1 presents a graphic view of Ghana's youth employment institutional structure, highlighting the various entities and the potential for duplication of effort.

FIGURE 3.1

Institutional structure of youth employment, Ghana

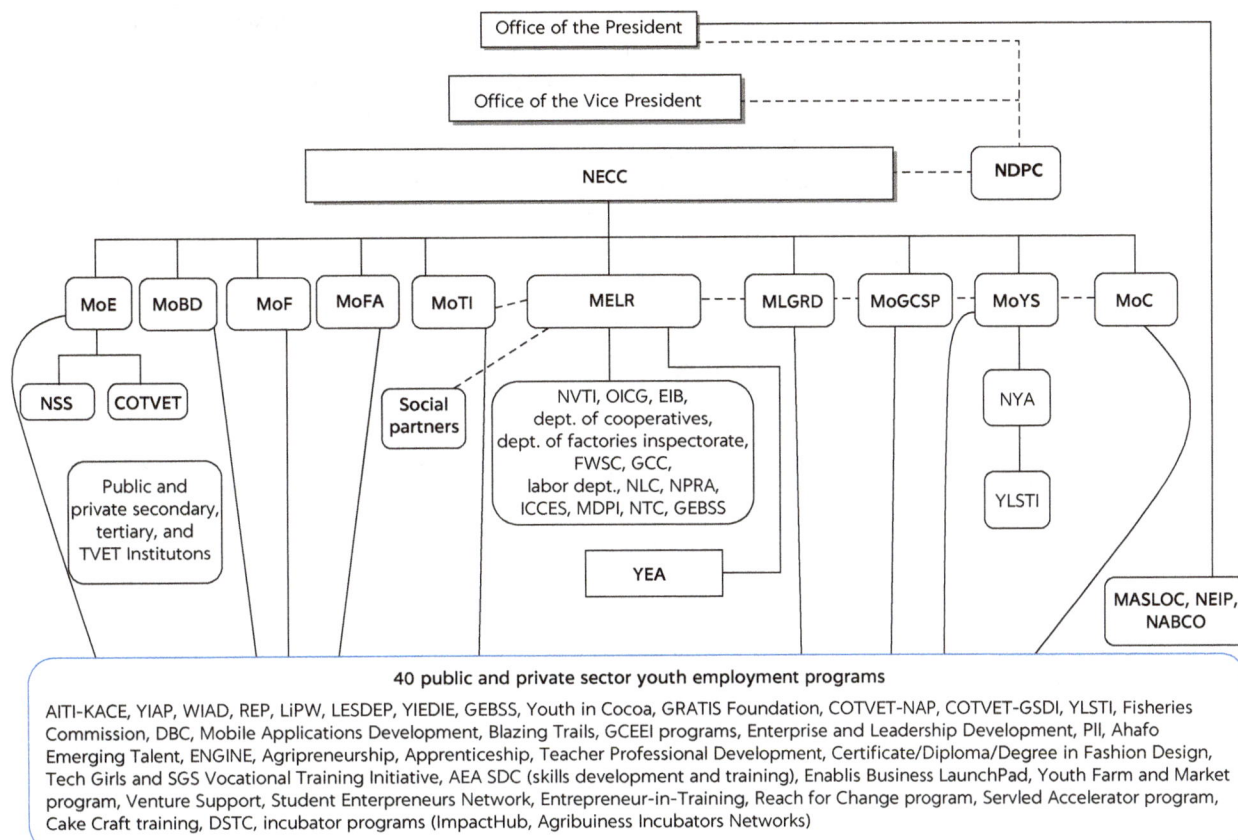

Source: World Bank.
Note: The National Employment Coordinating Council (NECC), proposed in National Employment Policy, is not yet functional. AAIT-KACE = Advanced Information Technology Institute–Kofi Annan Center of Excellence in ICT; AEA-SDC = African Entrepreneurship Academy–Skills Development Center; COTVET-GSDI = Council for Technical and Vocational Education and Training–Ghana Skills Development Initiative; COTVET-NAP = Council for Technical and Vocational Education and Training–National Apprenticeship Programme; DBC = Diploma in Business Consulting; DSTC = Deng Solar Training Center; EIB = Employment Information Bureau; ENGINE = Enhancing Growth in New Enterprises; FWSC = Fair Wages and Salaries Commission; GCC = Ghana Chamber of Commerce; GCEEI = Ghana Centre for Entrepreneurship Employment and Innovation; GEBSS = Graduate Business Support Scheme; ICCES = Integrated Community Centre for Employable Skills; LESDEP = Local Enterprise Skills Development Programme; LiPW = Labour-Intensive Public Works; MASLOC = Microfinance and Small Loans Centre; MDPI = Management Development and Productivity Institute; MELR = Ministry of Employment and Labour Relations; MLGRD = Ministry of Local Government and Rural Development; MoBD = Ministry of Business Development; MoC = Ministry of Communication; MoE = Ministry of Education; MoF = Ministry of Finance; MoFA = Ministry of Food and Agriculture; MoGCSP = Ministry of Gender, Children, and Social Protection; MoTI Ministry of Trade and Industry; MoYS = Ministry of Youth and Sports; NABCO = Nation Builders Corps; NDPC = National Development Planning Commission; NECC = National Employment Coordinating Council; NEIP = National Entrepreneurship and Innovation Programme; NLC = National Labour Commission; NPRA= National Pensions Regulatory Authority; NSS = National Service Scheme; NTC = National Tripartite Committee; NVTI = National Vocational Training Institute; NYA = National Youth Authority; OICG = Opportunities Industrialization Centre, Ghana; PII = Phinklife Institute Initiative; REP = Rural Enterprises Programme; TVET = technical and vocational education and training; WIAD = Women in Agricultural Development Directorate; YEA = Youth Employment Agency; YIAP = Youth in Agriculture Programme; YIEDIE = Youth Inclusive Entrepreneurial Development Initiative for Employment; YLSTI = Youth Leadership and Skills Training Institute.

NOTES

1. "Social partners" refer to organizations or entities—such as employers, trade unions, or employees—that participate in a cooperative relationship for the mutual benefit of all concerned. In Ghana, these are employers and organized labor.
2. See https://www.decentjobsforyouth.org/strategy.
3. The National Employment Policy proposes that the National Employment Coordinating Council be established and chaired by the vice president of Ghana to support implementation of the policy. The NECC has not yet been established.

REFERENCES

Ghana Ministry of Employment and Labour Relations. 2014. *National Employment Policy.* Accra: Ministry of Employment and Labour Relations. http://www.melr.gov.gh/wp-content /uploads/2015/12/National-Employment-Policy-2015.pdf.

Ghana Ministry of Gender, Children, and Social Protection. 2015. "National Social Protection Policy." Accra.

Ghana Ministry of Youth and Sports. 2014. "National Youth Policy Implementation Plan." Ghana Ministry of Youth and Sports, Accra.

4 Review of Youth Employment Programs in Ghana

PRIMARY YOUTH EMPLOYMENT INTERVENTIONS

Over the years, Ghana has implemented many youth employment interventions through the government, the private sector, and civil society and nongovernmental organizations. Meanwhile, public-private partnerships in youth employment remain limited, and current policies do not define clearly the role of the private sector. A best-case scenario would be one in which the private sector complements the government's job creation efforts. The perspectives of the private sector are therefore critical when developing strategies for youth employment. This section gives an overview of Ghana's existing youth employment programs and their shortcomings and the inherent opportunities for decent employment and job creation (see appendix A for profiles of the youth employment programs referenced in this study).

The youth employment program inventory carried out in 2016 by the World Bank (Avura and Ulzen-Appiah 2016) revealed that in Ghana, programs are highly focused on skills development and entrepreneurship training, and apprenticeships are commonplace. Public sector programs have a broader outreach and lower unit cost than private sector programs. The World Bank found that out of a pool of 145,000 applicants, only 29 percent gained access to programs run by nongovernmental organizations and private institutes. In the public sector, entry was even more restrictive; only 19 percent of approximately 1.3 million youth were accepted (Avura and Ulzen-Appiah 2016). Private sector programs, which focus mostly on skills and entrepreneurship training, tend to be more expensive and operate on a smaller scale relative to public sector programs. In general, the empirical data on the impact of both public and private sector programs are not available because evaluations have not been done. Moreover, tracer studies, which provide information on beneficiaries after they exit the program, have not been conducted for most programs or are not available to assist in evaluating the impact of programs. Information on cost parameters, such as cost per trainee and operational and investment costs over the program durations, are also limited. This gap needs to be addressed.

The main government programs that address youth unemployment (both short term and long term) are the following:

- Youth Employment Agency (YEA)
- National Vocational Training Institute (NVTI)
- Opportunities Industrialization Centre Ghana (OICG)
- Youth Leadership and Skills Training Institute
- Youth in Agriculture Programme (YIAP)
- National Entrepreneurship Innovation Programme (NEIP), previously Youth Enterprise Support (YES)
- Rural Enterprises Programme (REP)
- National Service Scheme (NSS)
- Nation Builders Corps (NABCO)

In terms of outreach and funding, the Youth Employment Agency and Nation Builders Corps are the largest programs, each engaging close to 100,000 youth annually. The government funds both programs, which have nationwide coverage.

In the absence of an impact evaluation of the youth employment programs, a strengths weaknesses, opportunities, and threats (SWOT) analysis was undertaken, based on the inventory of existing public and private programs (see figures 4.1 and 4.2).

FIGURE 4.1

SWOT analysis of public youth employment programs, Ghana

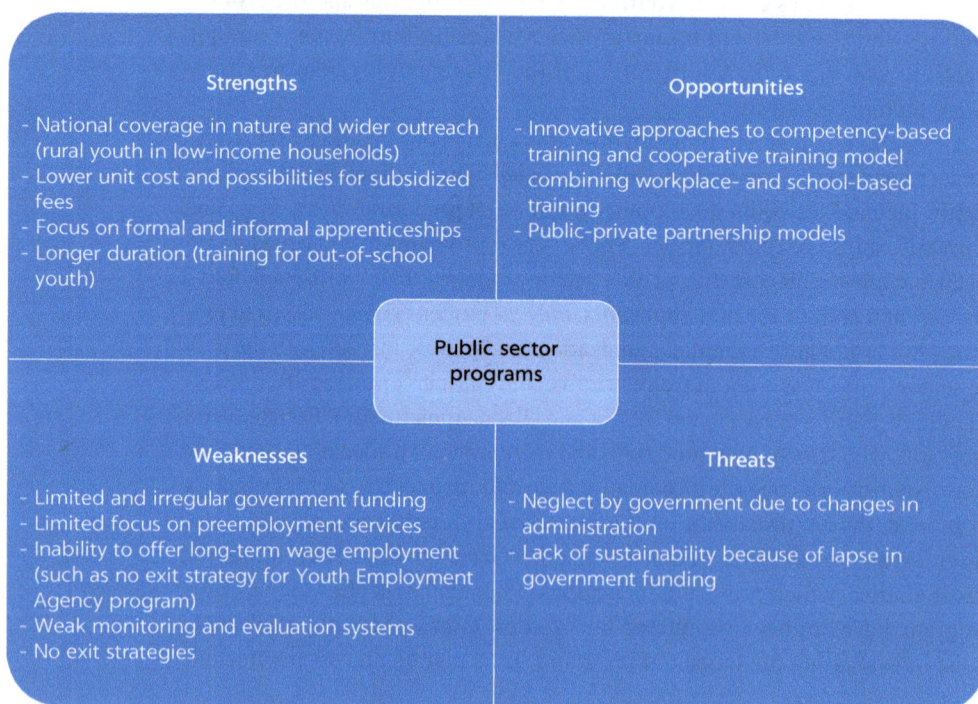

Strengths
- National coverage in nature and wider outreach (rural youth in low-income households)
- Lower unit cost and possibilities for subsidized fees
- Focus on formal and informal apprenticeships
- Longer duration (training for out-of-school youth)

Opportunities
- Innovative approaches to competency-based training and cooperative training model combining workplace- and school-based training
- Public-private partnership models

Public sector programs

Weaknesses
- Limited and irregular government funding
- Limited focus on preemployment services
- Inability to offer long-term wage employment (such as no exit strategy for Youth Employment Agency program)
- Weak monitoring and evaluation systems
- No exit strategies

Threats
- Neglect by government due to changes in administration
- Lack of sustainability because of lapse in government funding

Source: World Bank.
Note: SWOT = strengths, weakness, opportunities, and threats.

FIGURE 4.2

SWOT analysis of private youth employment programs, Ghana

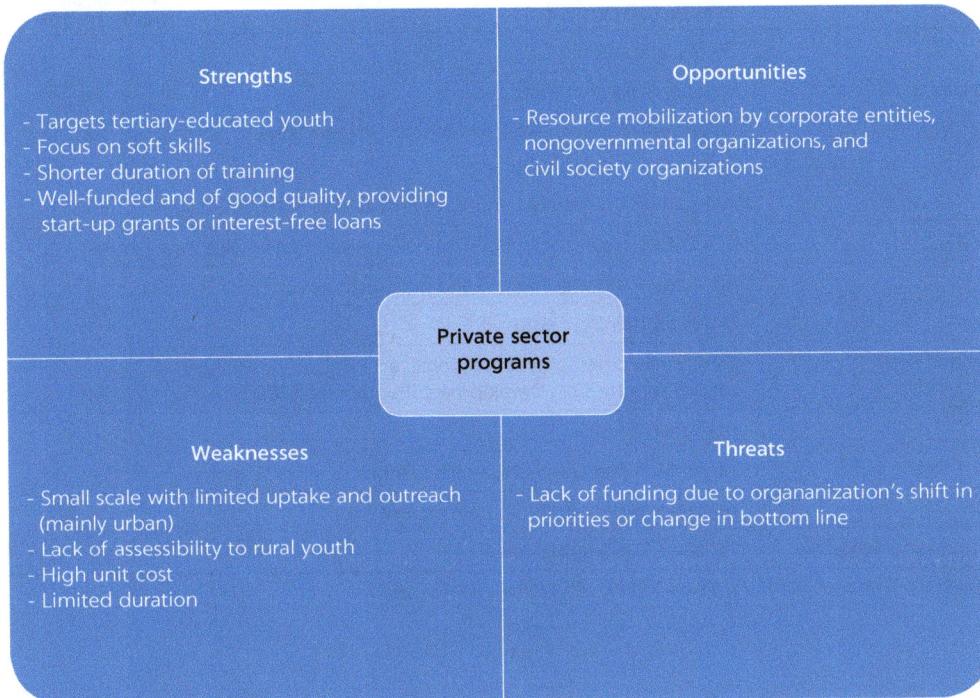

Strengths
- Targets tertiary-educated youth
- Focus on soft skills
- Shorter duration of training
- Well-funded and of good quality, providing start-up grants or interest-free loans

Opportunities
- Resource mobilization by corporate entities, nongovernmental organizations, and civil society organizations

Private sector programs

Weaknesses
- Small scale with limited uptake and outreach (mainly urban)
- Lack of assessibility to rural youth
- High unit cost
- Limited duration

Threats
- Lack of funding due to organanization's shift in priorities or change in bottom line

Source: World Bank.
Note: SWOT = strengths, weakness, opportunities, and threats.

TECHNICAL AND VOCATIONAL SKILLS TRAINING PROGRAMS

After being neglected for decades, Ghana's technical and vocational skills development programs have undergone a series of reforms since the 1970s. Effective vocational training programs can contribute significantly to worker productivity and economic growth, and since 2001 authorities have renewed the focus on skills development and its capacity to address unemployment. These institutions present an opportunity to offer training aimed at self-employment for out-of-school youth (junior high and high school dropouts) who are unable to further their education (Baffour-Awuah and Thompson 2011). Stakeholders indicated during consultations that demand for technical and vocational training has recently been growing among graduates of tertiary institutions who want to enhance their employability. In response to these needs and to position the technical and vocational education and training (TVET) sector appropriately to boost economic development, the government has developed the Strategic Plan for TVET Transformation to help the country develop a well-organized, coordinated, and effective national TVET system (Ghana Ministry of Education 2018).

In Ghana, TVET is offered at the pretertiary and tertiary levels in the forms of prevocational, vocational, and technical training. Prevocational training takes place at the basic level and aims to stimulate students' interest in vocational subjects and to equip them with basic skills in these subjects. At the tertiary level, education and training are provided by polytechnics and other institutions in the tertiary subsector. Currently, such training is delivered by different entities:

TABLE 4.1 **TVET institutions, Ghana**

MINISTRY	TYPE OF INSTITUTION	NUMBER OF INSTITUTIONS
Ministry of Education	Technical institutes	37
Ministry of Employment and Labour Relations	Vocational training institutes	34
	Opportunity Industrialization Centres, Ghana (OICG)	3
	Leadership training programs	9
	Integrated Community Centres for Employable Skills (ICCES)	63
Ministry of Trade and Industry	Ghana Regional Appropriate Technology Industrial Service	9
Ministry of Agriculture	Agricultural training colleges and farm institutes	3
Ministry of Road and Transport	Technical Training Centre	1
Ministry of Local Government and Rural Development	Community development vocational technical institutes under Local Enterprise Skills Development Programme (LESDEP)	24
Ministry of Tourism	Hospitality schools	—
Ministry of Communications	Information and communications technology (ICT) schools	—
Ministry of Youth and Sports	Youth leadership and skills training institutes	11
Ministry of Gender, Children, and Social Protection	Social welfare training centers	18

Sources: Adapted from Baffour-Awuah and Thompson (2011) and Ghana Ministry of Education (2018).
Note: — = not available.

multiple ministries, private for-profit and nonprofit institutes, and nongovernmental organizations, as well as through informal apprenticeships offered on an individual basis. Table 4.1 provides a breakdown of the multiple ministries that currently have a TVET connection and their respective institutions.

TVET delivery in Ghana is regulated, coordinated, and supervised at the national level by the Council for Technical and Vocational Education and Training (COTVET). COTVET was set up in 2006 with a mandate to formulate national policies for skills development across the broad spectrum of pretertiary and tertiary education and the formal, informal, and nonformal sectors. COTVET coordinates and supervises the activities of public and private providers, including apprenticeships in the informal sector. The council is also responsible for supporting the development of standards, validating learning and teaching materials, and mapping out the skills requirements for growth sectors, including scarce skills, as well as emphasizing the use of competency-based training strategies and skills for industry.

COTVET has implemented many projects aimed at improving the overall coordination and quality of the TVET sector. Under the Ghana Skills and Technology Development Project (GSTDP), which is funded by the World Bank and the Denmark Development Cooperation (DANIDA), reforms have addressed sustainable funding, government commitment, resource and infrastructure improvement, career guidance and counseling, high-quality assurance, and improvements in the public's perception of TVET. COTVET has developed many frameworks, including the National TVET Strategic Plan, which is aimed at helping to equip the country's workforce with the skills needed to drive and sustain industries.

Challenges confronting the TVET sector include limited numbers of technical institutes, lack of facilities and materials for training students, lack of competent technical instructors, widespread concern about poor-quality training and training environments, and difficulty in career progression for TVET students.

Linkages to technology and applied research through industry are still limited, and there is a mismatch between skills training and industry needs. COTVET has initiated skills gap assessments in various sectors to ensure that programs are relevant in a fast-changing global work environment that is increasingly dominated by the use of technology, and that the programs themselves and the training they offer meet the standards required by industry. However, more investments are needed to finance construction, as well as to revamp the equipment and tools available to existing vocational training institutions.

The budgets allocated by the government to the TVET sector are limited. According to reports, as of 2011 only 1 percent of the education budget of the Ministry of Education was allocated to the TVET subsector (Baffour-Awuah and Thompson 2011). In 2015 the allocation was 2.3 percent, an improvement over previous years (Ministry of Education 2016). However, external funding for the sector has improved substantially in recent years. Investments by the Ghana Skills and Technology Development Project totaled US$70 million over five years.[1] The subsequent Skills Development Fund (SDF) supported by DANIDA is investing US$14 million in the sector. The Skills Development Fund is expected in the medium term to become the government's principal instrument for financially supporting skills and technology innovation. COTVET has also received support from other development partners—such as the African Development Bank, the Japan International Cooperation Agency (JICA), the German development bank Kreditanstalt für Wiederaufbau (KFW), and the German development agency GIZ—to support the government's TVET reform efforts and to support development of the high-quality, mid-level technical and vocational skills needed in the Ghanaian economy.

Some of the existing public sector programs have skills training components, but they would require additional funding to reach more beneficiaries and would need to expand their scope to be most relevant. According to findings from stakeholder consultations, the sectors in which effective skills development could produce economic gains include transportation, hospitality and tourism, construction, agriculture, vehicle repair, fashion design, electronics, and electrical works.

APPRENTICESHIP PROGRAMS

Apprenticeship in Ghana has evolved over the past four decades since the establishment of the National Vocational Training Institute. The government's educational reform white paper identified apprenticeship as a track for post–basic education (Ghana Ministry of Education 2004). Apprenticeships prepare youth for self-employment or potential wage employment if they are hired by a master craftsperson through exposure to on-the-job learning of job-relevant skills. Apprenticeships are widespread in Ghana, normally targeting junior and senior high school graduates who have not had an opportunity to progress to the next level of education.

Formal apprenticeships are run by institutions including the National Vocational Training Institute, Opportunities Industrialization Centre Ghana, and other TVET institutions. The traditional informal apprenticeship system is often driven by the informal sector. Informal apprenticeship training accounts for 80–90 percent of all basic skills training in Ghana, compared with 5–10 percent by public training institutions and 10–15 percent by nongovernmental organizations and for-profit and nonprofit providers (Palmer 2009). Graduates of informal apprenticeships have two options for obtaining their certification: (1) certification by the Informal Sector Association or (2) a proficiency certificate issued by the National Vocational Training Institute that requires passing a nonwritten, competency-based skill test.

Ghana's apprenticeship program faces several key challenges. These include a limited number of formal vocational or technical institutes, lack of access by these institutes to technology upgrades, and promotion of entrepreneurial skills as part of their training. To address issues of standardization of training, COTVET introduced the National Apprenticeship Programme (NAP) as a pilot program in 2012. An evaluation of the program showed that (1) uptake and completion of apprenticeship programs differ by gender; (2) access to apprenticeship programs reduced wage employment for men and women and increased self-employment in some groups, particularly among women in the beauty sector; (3) no gains in earnings were found in the short run; and (4) apprenticeship programs can provide youth with skills, and they may encourage youth to shift into self-employment (Mbiti et al. 2019). In the meantime, improved apprenticeship models are being implemented through projects such as the Youth Inclusive Entrepreneurial Development Initiative for Employment (YIEDIE), the Ghana TVET Voucher Project, and the Apprenticeship to Entrepreneurship Project implemented by the National Board for Small Scale Industries (NBSSI). The impact of these programs has yet to be evaluated.

ENTREPRENEURSHIP TRAINING PROGRAMS

Entrepreneurship plays a vital role in job creation because it provides employment opportunities for young people. National development planning policies and strategies have identified youth entrepreneurship as an effective engine for economic development. The National Employment Policy proposes introducing support measures to provide special assistance for entrepreneurship development, particularly among women.

Research has demonstrated that, globally, entrepreneurship is indispensable to addressing youth unemployment, particularly for the category of youth who are not inclined to have "job-for-life" careers. Entrepreneurship programs have a higher impact in terms of employment creation (self-employment) than labor earnings (Cho and Honorati 2013; Kluve et al. 2016). Because Ghana's economy has slowed in recent years, promoting entrepreneurial activity can help at the macro level by contributing to the gross domestic product and at the micro level by creating stable and sustainable employment for young people.

Any business start-up needs financial, human, technological, and physical assets. Thus it is essential to have support structures in place to help start-ups acquire such resources to facilitate the business development process. Access to finance is a major challenge for would-be entrepreneurs in Ghana. Most youth lack savings, connections, and knowledge about where and how to secure funding. These issues emerged during discussions in almost all the stakeholder consultations. Start-up funds, such as grants and interest-free loans, support young people trying to launch businesses. However, many programs targeting youth do not provide enough support or information on how to secure funding.

Consultations also revealed that entrepreneurship training programs would be most effective for employment creation among both urban and rural youth if they include group concepts and leverage cooperatives.

Government agencies that promote youth entrepreneurship in Ghana include the National Youth Authority, Youth Employment Agency, National Entrepreneurship and Innovation Programme, National Board for Small Scale Industries, vocational and technical training centers, and microfinance programs, such as the Microfinance and Small Loans Centre. These institutions have a presence at the regional, metropolitan, municipal, and district levels. Elements of the entrepreneurship programs include provision of business advisory services, start-up kits, development of networking skills, support to access financing, and coaching and mentoring. Many of the programs do not provide support or follow-up services for beneficiaries.

In July 2017, the government launched the National Entrepreneurship and Innovation Programme (NEIP) with seed funding of $100 million under the Ministry of Business Development to meet the financing needs of young entrepreneurs who enroll in the program. This multifaceted initiative includes an incubator program for potential entrepreneurs, financing and business development services, and advisory services on how to gain access to markets, among other things. This program replaces the Youth Enterprise Support program. Four modules have been developed under the NEIP initiative: a business incubation program, an NEIP industrialization plan, the Youth Enterprise Fund (YEF), and business advisory services.

Private sector entrepreneurship initiatives include programs such as the Enhancing Growth in New Enterprises (ENGINE) project, the entrepreneurship program of the Campaign for Female Education (CAMFED), the Enablis Ghana program, Impact Hub, and the Ghana Climate Innovation Centre (GCIC). Most private sector programs are well funded and of high quality. They provide competitive start-up grants and loans, mentorship, international exposure, and other business advisory services to beneficiaries. They target tertiary-level graduates but have limited reach and coverage.

PREEMPLOYMENT SUPPORT SERVICES

Preemployment support is a critical element in preparing young people for the world of work. It covers career guidance and counseling, work-based learning, job search assistance, coaching, and mentoring. The goal of guidance and counseling is to enable young people to see and explore their full potential, help individuals to identify and learn the skills that will enable them to be more effective in planning for and choosing jobs, make effective transitions and adjustments to work, and well manage careers and career transitions.

Young people are most effective at work when they are exposed to realistic views of different career paths. They have an opportunity to receive such exposure by spending some time in workplaces through work-based learning. This type of learning, as noted, is often seen as essential for developing workplace skills and promoting the productivity of the labor force. This approach also strengthens hard and soft skills, offers vital workplace knowledge and experience, and instills positive work habits. Research has shown that work-based learning has a positive correlation with higher wages and effectively supports transitions from school to work, leading to high-quality jobs and career pathways. For employers, work-based learning can help to address skills gaps, support effective talent recruitment, enhance employee retention and satisfaction, and increase overall productivity (Raelin 2008).

Preemployment support services are mostly inadequate and ineffective in Ghana, particularly in public training and academic institutions. The Ghana Education Service (GES) and most tertiary-level educational institutions in Ghana have guidance and counseling units intended to provide support for students. Public vocational and technical institutions also offer some services. However, the effectiveness of these units is limited, and they tend to not provide prolonged coaching and mentoring. Thus youth are mostly left up to their own devices in terms of career development, often resulting in decisions based on peer pressure and trends instead of choosing jobs based on individual talents, strengths, and competencies. This gap in preemployment services exists in all spheres of the educational system. Stakeholder consultations confirmed that funding for preemployment support is minimal.

Identifying internships for students during their tertiary education is a growing trend. Ashesi University, for example, has designed a comprehensive preemployment support structure that offers students services throughout all four years of college. The program integrates guidance and counseling, internships, coaching, and mentoring, and focuses students on ethics, civic engagement, and the development of leadership skills and technological competencies. The goal is to prepare students to be globally competitive with respect to employment. This model also integrates entrepreneurship to help students develop an entrepreneurial mind-set, thereby enhancing their employability. Ashesi University reports successful results, with 94 percent of graduates finding jobs within six months of graduation. This model could be studied further with the intention of replicating it in public tertiary institutions. However, one likely challenge would be funding.

As for job search assistance, the Employment Information Bureau (EIB) of the Department of Labour at the Ministry of Employment and Labour Relations (MELR) is the government agency responsible for providing such services. It disseminates occupational information through school visits, makes referrals for training and skills development, and facilitates registration and placement in jobs. EIB has 64 public employment centers in 38 districts across the country to help youth learn about the availability and suitability of jobs. The agency, in collaboration with key stakeholders such as the Ghana Statistical Service and the Ghana Immigration Service, has received support from the World Bank to develop the Ghana Labour Market Information System (GLMIS). This integrated online platform seeks to improve information flow between the demand and supply sides of the labor market. The system has been piloted but is not yet fully operational.

Stakeholder consultations revealed that the impact of the public employment centers is hardly felt by youth across the country, in part because of their limited number, but even more so because of the very limited human capacity within these centers. Furthermore, EIB lacks adequate funding, staffing, and logistics to meet the country's labor market information management needs. New funding from the European Union and the World Bank in 2020 will be critical for improving the effectiveness of the public employment centers and the availability of labor market data nationwide.

NOTE

1. GSTDP was funded by the World Bank and DANIDA.

REFERENCES

Avura, Francis Babongte, and Ato Ulzen-Appiah. 2016. *An Inventory of Youth Employment Programmes in Ghana*. Accra: World Bank.

Baffour-Awuah, Daniel, and Samuel Thompson. 2011. "A Holistic Approach to Technical and Vocational Skills Development (TVSD) Policy and Governance Reform: The Case of Ghana." Paper presented at ADEA Triennale on Education and Training in Africa, Ouagadougou, Burkina Faso, November 27–December 2.

Cho, Yoonyoung, and Maddalena Honorati. 2013. "Entrepreneurship Programs in Developing Countries: A Meta Regression Analysis." Policy Research Working Paper 6402, World Bank, Washington, DC.

Ghana Ministry of Education. 2004. "White Paper on the Report of the Education Reform Review Committee." Accra.

Ghana Ministry of Education. 2018. *Strategic Plan for TVET Transformation, 2018–2022*. Council for Technical and Vocational Education and Training, Accra.

Kluve, Jochen, Susana Puerto, David Robalino, Jose Manuel Romero, Friederike Rother, Jonathan Stöterau, Felix Weidenkaff, et al. 2016. "Do Youth Employment Programs Improve Labor Market Outcomes? A Systematic Review." Discussion Paper 10263, IZA, Bonn.

Mbiti, Isaac, Jamie McCasland, Morgan Hardy, Kym Cole, Mark Enriquez, and Isabelle Salcher. 2019. "Training for Success: Targeting and Incentives in Apprenticeship Training in Ghana." 3ie Grantee Final Report, International Initiative for Impact Evaluation (3ie), New Delhi.

Palmer, Robert. 2009. "Formalising the Informal: Ghana's National Apprenticeship Programme." *Journal of Vocational Education and Training* 61 (1): 67–83.

Raelin, Joseph. 2008. *Work-Based Learning: Bridging Knowledge and Action in the Workplace*. Rev. ed. San Francisco: John Wiley / Jossey-Bass.

5 Options for Youth Employment in Ghana

This chapter focuses on opportunities and options identified for addressing youth employment in Ghana based on existing programs, global and regional lessons reviewed in the previous chapter, and proposals gathered through a series of stakeholder consultations. The chapter also highlights possible strategies for different categories of youth, with possible options for employment and decent work in Ghana.

DEFINING OPTIONS FOR YOUTH EMPLOYMENT IN GHANA

A key employment issue for Ghana is the lack of productivity, which leads to low earnings. The biggest challenge is therefore finding ways to create productive employment, as well as decent jobs with sustainable earnings.

Evidence suggests that the first step in developing effective youth employment approaches is to conduct an analysis of the economy and the inherent potential employment opportunities. In most cases, those opportunities will be in the same sectors as in the past, with some shifts toward new sectors and emerging activities. Opportunities for youth are a function of the overall set of employment opportunities in a country. Interventions to help youth enter the labor force and find sustainable livelihoods therefore must recognize this reality (Fox and Kaul 2017). To facilitate entry, improve productivity, and raise earnings across the range of employment in agriculture, household enterprises, and the modern wage sector, the most pressing priority is to ensure that the educational system delivers high-quality learning and skills. Other important priorities are to identify and build the socioemotional and behavioral skills that contribute to productivity, including the skills demanded by employers (Filmer and Fox 2014).

Both supply-side and demand-side factors should be addressed when designing youth employment interventions. Demand-side interventions could focus on promoting company growth and job creation through activities such as management training, mentoring, and incubation services, which raise the profitability of and expand firms; greater access to financing; a reduction in corporate taxation; investment in infrastructure to support firm entry and growth; and employment subsidies to encourage firms to hire youth. Supply-side interventions could focus on helping youth enter the labor market through skills training, including vocational and technical skills, business skills for self-employment and employability, and noncognitive skills. Other services that could help youth find and keep jobs include counseling and mentoring services for either self- or wage employment and the provision of labor market information.

Systematic reviews have found that programs implemented by public sector agencies enjoy less success than those implemented by nongovernmental organizations (NGOs) or the private sector (Kluve et al. 2016). Yet NGOs often lack the administrative capacity and financial resources to bring programs to scale. A hybrid approach is therefore suggested. Ghana could test this proposition by considering more public-private partnership models for youth employment.

Any options for young people seeking jobs must include consideration of the disparity in unemployment and literacy rates between urban and rural areas. The unemployment rate in urban areas (13.4 percent) is relatively higher than that in rural areas (10.2 percent), irrespective of gender. The urban unemployment rate is higher than the rural unemployment rate in 7 of Ghana's 10 regions, except in the Greater Accra, Ashanti, and Upper East regions, where the trend is different (Ghana Statistical Service 2015). The northern regions have the lowest youth literacy rates for both females (31.9 percent) and males (50.6 percent).[1] Proposed intervention options and designs need to factor in these statistics. Also, policy makers and other stakeholders should pay special attention when designing interventions for youth employment in the northern regions of Ghana because these regions have comparatively lower youth literacy rates.

To effectively address youth unemployment and underemployment, it is important to categorize youth to better address each group's particular needs. For the purposes of this report. youth have been placed in the following categories: (1) uneducated youth in rural areas; (2) uneducated youth in urban areas; (3) educated youth (secondary) in rural areas; (4) educated youth (secondary) in urban areas; (5) educated youth (tertiary) in rural areas; and (6i) educated youth in urban areas. Table 5.1 describes these categories of youth.

TABLE 5.1 Youth categories and their characteristics, Ghana

UNEDUCATED YOUTH IN RURAL AREAS	UNEDUCATED YOUTH IN URBAN AREAS	EDUCATED YOUTH (SECONDARY) IN RURAL AREAS	EDUCATED YOUTH (SECONDARY) IN URBAN AREAS	EDUCATED YOUTH (TERTIARY) IN RURAL AREAS	EDUCATED YOUTH (TERTIARY) IN URBAN AREAS
• Constitute 21 percent of youth population in rural areas • Have insufficient access to high-quality education and sustainable livelihoods • Are mostly poor because of their location • Tend to be self-employed and work in agriculture (mostly subsistence farming) or are farm-hands employed by large farms	• Constitute 10.6 percent of youth in urban areas • Often find work in street vending • Put less focus on farm activities • Tend to work in the service and private wage sectors	• Constitute 71.3 percent of youth in rural areas • Tend to migrate to urban areas • Have limited opportunities to start an agribusiness or add value to crops • Are limited by poor infrastructure, lack of processing and storage facilities, weak cooperatives, and lack of market access • Are not attracted to subsistence agriculture	• Constitute 71.3 percent of youth in urban areas • Tend to engage in menial jobs and be active in informal sector	• Constitute 2.7 percent of youth in rural areas • Made up of more males (5.4 percent) than females (2.6 percent)	• Constitute 8.6 percent of youth in urban areas • Include more males (5.4 percent) than females (2.6 percent) • Have capacity to develop enterprises in productive sectors

Sources: Compiled from Ghana Statistics Service (2016, 2018).

Note: Youth are ages 15–35. The total youth population based on the GLSS 7 report is estimated at 34.2 percent, or approximately 9.7 million of the estimated population of 28 million (Ghana Statistics Service 2018). In the GLSS 7 report, Ghana reported the "relaxed" version of unemployment, which defines a person as unemployed if "he/she was not engaged in any work, had no attachment to a job or business and was 'potentially' available for jobs." "Uneducated" refers to persons with no education up to primary education. "Secondary" includes persons with up to a junior high school, middle school, senior high school, or secondary education (see https://education.stateuniversity.com/pages/533/Ghana-secondary-education.html). "Tertiary" includes persons with a university (bachelor's or postgraduate) degree. "Educated" refers to persons with a secondary or higher education.

Youth with up to a university education constitute 80.9 percent of youth in urban areas and 19.1 percent in rural areas. Rural areas are home to 45.5 percent of the youth population, and the rural youth unemployment rate is estimated at 12.6 percent. Urban areas are home to 54.3 percent of the youth population, and the urban youth unemployment rate is 15.8 percent.

PROPOSED PRIORITY AREAS OF FOCUS

When policy makers are deciding what kind of youth employment interventions to adopt, it is important to consider the expected job outcomes for program participants. This decision will then determine the kind of investments required. For many youth employment programs, the objective is often to provide transitional employment options and not full-time, longer-term employment. In Ghana, policy makers need to take into account the country's current high unemployment rate and the limitations on expanding public sector employment, which rule out the public sector as a long-term vehicle for job creation. In view of this situation, realistic short- to medium-term job outcomes might be defined as supporting youth to transition from unemployment or underemployment into productive self-employment or helping self-employed youth maintain an existing business over the medium to long terms. Currently, the majority of young people in self-employment (own-account workers and unpaid family workers) are among the poorest paid workers in Ghana's informal economy (Ghana Statistical Service 2015).

Stakeholder consultations and reviews point to five priority areas that could potentially create employment opportunities for Ghanaian youth. The options posited are not new areas of youth employment in Ghana. Rather, the idea is to maximize their inherent potential impact by scaling up existing interventions and improving their capacity for outreach. The five priority areas are

- Promoting agriculture and agribusiness
- Apprenticeship (skills training)
- Promoting entrepreneurship
- Other high-yielding areas (renewable energy–solar, construction, tourism, sports, and green jobs)
- Preemployment support services

These areas are described in the following sections. Cross-cutting areas of attention include harnessing research and technology; gender mainstreaming; ensuring decent work for all people, including the vulnerable; creating access to finance; ensuring programs are driven by the private sector; and, above all, providing effective coordination among all youth employment programs.

Promoting agriculture and agribusiness

Although the agriculture sector has been overtaken by the service sector in recent years, it still contributes significantly to the Ghanaian economy. The sector employs more than 50 percent of the population and still holds enormous opportunities for employment creation for youth. Evidence suggests that the sector remains a main gateway to work, and that, for many, it will become the sector of lifetime employment. Thus if productivity and earnings in agriculture do not improve, the wider economy will remain depressed in rural areas, where the majority of the population lives, and options for youth will shrink (Filmer and Fox 2014).

In terms of work, rural youth are more likely to be engaged in agriculture, fisheries, forestry, handicrafts, small-scale retail (microenterprises), or cottage industry. Prospects in the agriculture sector for young people include agroprocessing; cultural practice services in areas such as disease, pest, and weed control services; transportation; agricultural waste conversion storage (warehousing); and organic farming.[2] Additional opportunities for youth could arise from linking farmers to markets or to machinery services. Young people also have the potential to engage in entrepreneurial and vocational training opportunities along the full length of the agricultural value chain (production to marketing), while for tertiary-level graduates, the sector today offers career opportunities in research, financial management, engineering, and other technical areas. To grow agribusinesses to scale, it is essential to develop technology hubs by working with universities and research institutions to establish business incubation centers (discussed in more detail later in this chapter).

Rural-educated youth are not attracted to low-productivity or subsistence agriculture. The absence of jobs in rural areas is a cause of the migration of youth to urban areas, where they seek nonagricultural jobs. The migration of young adults to cities can result in a shift in the age structure of the rural population toward older ages, with clear implications for labor markets, agricultural production, and food security. Meanwhile, youth in rural areas have few opportunities to add value to crops or to start agribusiness or agricultural entrepreneurial activities. They are limited by poor infrastructure, a lack of processing and storage facilities, weak cooperative groups, and poor access to markets and networking opportunities. As the sector that drives the rural economy in Ghana, agriculture needs to undergo massive transformation to create employment opportunities for youth.

Existing programs, such as the Rural Enterprises Programme (REP), could be scaled up to cover more districts. This program currently covers 161 of the 216 districts in Ghana. Moreover, the government has begun implementing the ENABLE Youth program in collaboration with the African Development Bank (AfDB). These programs, if well implemented, hold much promise for job creation for youth in agriculture. The Young Professionals for Agricultural Development (YPARD) in Ghana is quite active as well, and this network's efforts could be leveraged to promote more youth participation in agriculture.

Ghana has the human and institutional capacity to set up agriculture and agribusiness incubation centers (incubators are defined and discussed later in this chapter). Incubation centers may include vocational and technical schools, agricultural colleges and farms, universities, national and regional research centers, seed business development centers, incubators, hubs, and small and medium enterprise (SME) accelerators. The current human, institutional, policy, and physical infrastructure in Ghana offers great potential for agribusiness. For example, the REP reported supporting more than 20,000 entrepreneurs in 2014. But on the ground, the enterprises supported require more assistance, such as through mentorships, if they would like to expand their businesses.

According to the stakeholder discussions, Ghana has adopted a variety of approaches and models of agribusiness incubation. Research and higher institutions of learning, for example, have used science parks as incubation centers to help students become conversant with science and technology. To maximize their ability to create jobs, such institutions require clear, results-oriented goals for job creation. Partnerships with the private sector and implementation of market-driven approaches would be essential.

Apprenticeships (skills training)

Apprenticeships provide ample entrepreneurial and employment opportunities for youth, particularly those from poor households and rural areas, as well as women. However, based on public negative perceptions and the lack of information about the array of possibilities available through apprenticeships, most youth do not take advantage of this option. Research in Kenya, for example, has shown that young people typically have inaccurate perceptions of the returns on vocational training, including misconceptions about which trades provide the highest earnings (Hicks et al. 2011). The government therefore needs to make a concerted effort to change perceptions of apprenticeships to attract more youth to this area.

Most apprenticeship programs in Ghana are informal. The literature suggests that a combination of formal or informal technical skills training and on-the-job learning tends to have short- and long-term positive impacts on youth employment and earnings. Countries that have implemented combined programs include Colombia (Jovenes en Accion), the Dominican Republic (Juventud y Empleo), and Kenya (Youth Empowerment Programs). These programs have demonstrated a positive impact on paid employment and higher earnings at different rates for both males and female (Honorati 2016). Meanwhile, training should be broadened to focus not only on present needs but also on the future career perspectives of young people.

Most skills training programs and apprenticeships in Ghana have failed to be market-relevant because of the challenges noted earlier. Research has shown that providing skills alone has no effects on entrepreneurship because most trainees need start-up capital to set up their enterprises after training. For example, a young person seeking to launch a start-up in the agriculture sector, even one involving subsistence farming, will need land and capital. To make apprenticeships more relevant, programs should incorporate entrepreneurship training. The National Board for Small Scale Industries (NBSSI), for example, has implemented an apprenticeship-to -entrepreneurship model that incorporates entrepreneurial training within the apprenticeship program. Such a system could be explored as an option for increasing the capacity of apprentices to become effective entrepreneurs upon completion of their training.

Options for promoting entrepreneurship

Many young people across the world are enthusiastic about starting their own businesses, but they face many challenges. They lack savings, collateral for loans, know-how, and experience. Youth in Ghana need to be empowered through well-thought-out combinations of mentorship, coaching, skills development, entrepreneurship development, financial literacy, and access to financial services. They also need access to the appropriate technologies, good infrastructure and a capacity to conduct any needed assessments, as well as space for doing business. Overall, for entrepreneurship to thrive, the entire ecosystem needs to support businesses.

The Ministry of Business Development (MoBD) is championing the establishment of business incubation in partnership with the country's public universities. The government plans to establish four incubators, in Accra, Kumasi, Takoradi, and Tamale. Hopefully, these pilots can provide insight into what is effective in the Ghanaian context and open opportunities for scaling up.

Other high-yielding, job-creating areas

For anyone designing youth employment interventions, the importance of conducting a diagnosis of the economy to identify potential sectors for job growth cannot be understated. As the Ghanaian economy grows, different sectors will offer the potential for employment creation. Currently, the extractive industries (oil and gold) account for a large share of the country's growth, but these very specialized sectors produce only limited jobs. The government must diversify into other sectors to create a more inclusive growth strategy that generates more and productive jobs for all. To explore opportunities to diversify Ghana's economy, the Council for Technical and Vocational Education and Training (COTVET) has carried out a skills audit to guide future policy decisions. Indeed, policy makers should give priority to those sectors with a high potential to create jobs. They might also consider channeling resources from high-value-added sectors to sectors that are ripe for job creation as a way of making growth more inclusive. Sectors that could be explored include renewable energy (solar), construction, tourism, sports, and green technologies and practices. The specific opportunities in these sectors need to be researched to guide any future youth training programs.

Business incubation and job creation

One development that can boost all four areas discussed earlier—agriculture and agribusiness, apprenticeship, entrepreneurship, and high-yielding sectors such as tourism or construction—is incubators. The term *incubator* refers to a firm or enterprise whose focus is to nurture new business ventures or support existing or emerging businesses. Incubators seek to create a positive entrepreneurial environment that encourages and facilitates start-up survival and the growth of new business ventures. Business incubation programs are designed to promote the economic development of communities, groups, or individuals by supporting their business development (see the earlier example demonstrating the value of incubators in boosting the agriculture and agribusiness sector).

Research shows that globally, 80 percent of jobs are created by the informal private sector. Incubators offer services and products to support the informal and formal private sectors in the early stages of establishment and development. Services provided by incubators typically fall into five broad categories: (1) start-up consulting and business planning; (2) mentorship and coaching; (3) access to financing; (4) technology and innovation commercialization; and (5) market development. Ghana has a number of business incubators, but most are located in urban areas. For example, agribusiness incubation centers can be established in all districts in Ghana to serve as a stimulus for massive skills development that could cascade across all categories of youth. With more than 40 youth employment programs inventoried, the ecosystem is ready to absorb incubation models once the right policies are in place, resources are allocated, and the private sector is in the driver's seat. The creation of such incubators could also address some of the fragmentation and duplication issues within Ghana's youth employment arena by bringing together industries with similar goals and objectives to boost economies of scale.

Options for preemployment support services

The main complaint from employers across Africa about employing youth is that they lack "employable" skills and do not have technical skills (Filmer and Fox 2014). Yet several impact evaluations have shown that, by themselves, life skills programs do not increase employment rates. Perhaps these skills must be "learned while doing," which makes a case for internships and work-based learning. Recent research shows that workers need both technical skills and "soft" or behavioral skills to succeed. Employers should be closely involved in training to ensure that the skills provided are relevant to the labor market. However, the most effective means of teaching these skills to workers and the most effective mechanisms for engaging employers in skills development are still not clear.

Job requirements and skills profiles are changing rapidly due to industrialization and technological developments. Researchers have projected that, on average, by 2030 more than a third of the desired core skill sets of most occupations will comprise skills that are not yet considered crucial to the job today. Overall, social skills—such as persuasion, creativity, critical thinking, and emotional intelligence, rather than narrow technical skills, such as programming or equipment operation and control—will become more relevant (Bughin et al. 2018; World Economic Forum 2016).

Preemployment support provided under Ghana's educational system has not been effective in developing the employability and entrepreneurial talent of young people, so it is in need of urgent reform. The country's educational system is generally rigid and does not provide sufficient space for students to develop their interests and talents, including those in specific subject areas outside the usual subject combinations recommended by the Ghana Education Service (GES). This lack of flexibility limits young people's potential, and in the longer term it results in students who lack passion for what they are studying. To address this situation, education reforms should allow for broader options, and career guidance and counseling programs should be revamped to guide student choices. Funding could go toward establishing effective coaching and mentoring systems in educational institutions across the country and toward conducting a review of the overall educational system to explore ways to give young people greater flexibility in making career choices.

The preemployment support approach implemented by some private universities in Ghana offers a model for the rest of the country. This model integrates guidance and counseling, internships, coaching, and mentoring over the entire period of study by students. Public universities, which reach many more students, might consider adopting a similar approach, although that would require additional government funding.

In addition, educational institutes, especially public schools and universities, need to make a conscious effort to prepare students to transition smoothly into the world of work. A structured and comprehensive internship and work-based learning policy—covering job recruitment, intern remuneration, soft skills, work ethics, and values training—should be integrated into the educational system to prepare students for an effective school–work transition.

Currently, the number and capacity of public employment centers are grossly inadequate to address the growing needs of the country's entire labor market, and even more so those of the youth. Funding for these centers is also woefully inadequate. It is important to increase the number of such centers across the country, but also to ensure they are well resourced in terms of both infrastructure and human capacity. The government could consider adopting public-private partnership arrangements to set up more centers and establishing monitoring and evaluation systems to track their effectiveness and efficiency.

Other potential options

Ghana's Labour-Intensive Public Works (LiPW) program is a possibility for addressing short-term youth unemployment, particularly in rural areas. Public works programs provide short-term employment to rehabilitate public assets that improve the productivity of communities. Despite their short duration, these programs could provide immediate income support and open avenues for investment by poor individuals. In view of the positive experiences gained from implementation of the LiPW under the Ghana Social Opportunities Project (GSOP) over the past few years, opportunities for youth employment in rural areas could be explored.

Business cooperatives offer a viable option for enterprise development because they have lower failure rates than traditional firms and small businesses after the first year of starting up and after five years in business.[3] About 10 percent of cooperatives fail after the first year compared with 60–80 percent of traditional businesses (Nembhard 2014). In Ghana, the Department of Co-operatives under the Ministry of Employment and Labour Relations is working closely with cooperatives in the agriculture and industrial sectors. As of 2016, more than 11,000 cooperatives with memberships ranging from 190 to 300 were registered with the department. The department has proposed a business model to guide the operations of these cooperatives and is working to improve their performance. It will be useful to evaluate the effect of business cooperatives on promoting youth employment in Ghana.

Table 5.2 is a summary of intervention options for the five priority areas for facilitating youth job creation—promoting agriculture and agribusiness, apprenticeships, promoting entrepreneurship, other high-yielding areas, and preemployment support—broken down by the six categories of youth. The table is by no means exhaustive, and the options point to an emphasis on entrepreneurship, which may not be the most optimal solution. However, in view of the limitations in wage employment in the current country context, perhaps going in this direction is a realistic choice. Table 5.3 is an intervention matrix that could be used to guide policy implementation on youth employment.

TABLE 5.2 Intervention options for addressing youth employment, Ghana

PRIORITY AREA	UNEDUCATED YOUTH IN RURAL AREAS	UNEDUCATED YOUTH IN URBAN AREAS	EDUCATED YOUTH (SECONDARY) IN RURAL AREAS	EDUCATED YOUTH (SECONDARY) IN URBAN AREAS	EDUCATED YOUTH (TERTIARY) IN RURAL AREAS	EDUCATED YOUTH (TERTIARY) IN URBAN AREAS
Promoting agriculture and agribusiness	Productive agriculture Product aggregation and marketing	Agroprocessing and value addition Aggregator incubators	Bulking, logistics management Storage and supply chain management	Technology and innovation commercialization	Technology and innovation commercialization Commercial farming Value addition and processing business development	Social enterprise development technology and innovation business incubators Agroprocessing and value addition business incubators Agribusiness education and research for business development Seed business incubators
Apprenticeship	Skills training	Skills training in productive sectors	Skills training	Skills training	Skills training	
Promoting entrepreneurship	Agribusiness development	Enterprise development	Skills training Cooperative development	Business incubation Cooperative development	Agribusiness development	Research on business development services Seed production and marketing Value addition and business development Skills training
Other high-yielding areas	Productive public works		Skills training	Skills training	Skills training and enterprise development	Enterprise development (renewable energy, construction, tourism)
Preemployment support	Financial literacy Coaching and mentoring	Financial literacy Coaching and mentoring	Mentorship and coaching	Mentoring and coaching Financial literacy	Soft skills while in school	Soft skills while in school

Source: World Bank.

TABLE 5.3 **Youth employment intervention matrix, Ghana**

TARGET GROUP	POSSIBLE INTERVENTION	SOFT SKILL	INSTITUTION	LOCATION
Poor, uneducated youth	• Training for productive agriculture • Labour-Intensive Public Works • Productive inclusion • Agribusiness incubation	Mentoring Coaching Financial literacy	MLRD MELR MoGCSP MoFA Private sector MoBD MoTI	Rural
Uneducated youth	• Agribusiness incubation • Skills in agriculture • Apprenticeships • Enterprise development	Mentoring Coaching Financial literacy	Urban authorities MoFA Private sector MoTI MoBD	Urban
Educated youth (secondary)	• Entrepreneurship training • Apprenticeships • Vocational training • Enterprise development • Skills in agriculture • Agribusiness incubation	Preemployment support Mentoring Coaching Financial literacy	MLRD MELR MoGCSP MoFA MoTI MoBD Private sector	Rural
Educated youth (secondary)	• Entrepreneurship training • Apprenticeships • Vocational training • Enterprise development	Preemployment support Mentoring Coaching Financial literacy	MELR MoFA MoTI MoBD Urban authorities Private sector	Urban
Educated youth (tertiary)	• Agribusiness incubation • Entrepreneurship training • Enterprise development • Apprenticeships • Vocational training	Preemployment support Mentoring Coaching Financial literacy	MLRD MELR MoGCSP MoFA MoTI MoBD Private sector	Rural
Educated youth (tertiary)	• Agribusiness incubation • Entrepreneurship training • Enterprise development • Apprenticeships • Vocational training	Preemployment support Mentoring Coaching Financial literacy	Urban authorities MELR MoFA MoTI MoBD Private sector	Urban

Source: World Bank.
Note: MELR = Ministry of Employment and Labour Relations; MLRD = Ministry of Local Government and Rural Development; MoBD = Ministry of Business Development; MoFA = Ministry of Food and Agriculture; MoGCSP = Ministry of Gender, Children, and Social Protection; MoTI = Ministry of Trade and Industry.

NOTES

1. This Ghana Statistical Service (2015) report is based on past surveys and reports that covered the 10 regions of the country.
2. Cultural practices in farming are those measures taken to ensure the productivity of crops.
3. A cooperative is a private business organization that is owned and controlled by the people who use its products, supplies, or services. Although cooperatives vary in type and membership size, all are formed to meet the specific objectives of members. The benefits of cooperatives typically include pooling risk, an ability to make a large purchase in a group, and empowerment of members, who feel like they are part of a meaningful company.

REFERENCES

Bughin, Jacques, Eric Hazan, Paris Susan Lund, Peter Dahlström, Anna Wiesinger, and Amresh Subramaniam. 2018. "Skill Shift: Automation and the Future of the Workforce." Discussion paper, McKinsey & Company, Brussels.

Filmer, Deon, and Louise Fox. 2014. *Youth Employment in Sub-Saharan Africa*. Africa Development Series. Washington, DC: World Bank.

Fox, Louise, and Upaasna Kaul. 2017. "The Evidence Is In: How Should Youth Employment Programs in Low-Income Countries Be Designed?" U.S. Agency for International Development, Washington, DC.

Ghana Statistical Service. 2016. *2015 Labour Force Report*. Accra: Ghana Statistical Service.

Ghana Statistical Service. 2018. "Ghana Living Standards Survey Round 7 (GLSS 7). Poverty Trends in Ghana 2005–2017." Accra.

Hicks, Joan Hamory, Michael Kremer, Isaac Mbiti, and Edward Miguel. 2011. "Vocational Education Voucher Delivery and Labor Market Returns." Working paper, International Growth Centre, London.

Honorati, Maddalena. 2016. *Harnessing Youth Potential in Ghana: A Policy Note*. Washington, DC: World Bank.

Kluve, Jochen, Susana Puerto, David Robalino, Jose Manuel Romero, Friederike Rother, Jonathan Stöterau, Felix Weidenkaff, et al. 2016. "Do Youth Employment Programs Improve Labor Market Outcomes? A Systematic Review." Discussion Paper 10263, IZA, Bonn.

Nembhard, Jessica Gordon. 2014. "Benefits and Impacts of Cooperatives." *Grassroots Economic Organizing (GEO) Newsletter*, vol. 2, theme 18. http://www.geo.coop/story/benefits-and-impacts-cooperatives.

World Economic Forum. 2016. *The Future of Jobs: Employment, Skills and Workforce Strategy for the Fourth Industrial Revolution*. Geneva: World Economic Forum.

6 Cross-Cutting Themes

PLANNING, COORDINATION, MONITORING, AND EVALUATION

Ghana's youth employment scene is uncoordinated and fragmented, with overlaps in mandates among stakeholder institutions. A lack of synergies limits the effectiveness, efficiency, and overall impact of programming. In response, the National Employment Policy proposed the establishment by law of a National Employment Coordinating Council (NECC) to play an oversight role in planning and coordinating, and in measuring results. As proposed, the NECC would consist of representatives of employment creation sectors and social partner organizations. It would be chaired by the vice president of Ghana and coordinated by the Ministry of Employment and Labour Relations (MELR). As part of its responsibilities, the NECC would send monitoring and evaluation reports annually to the president, cabinet, ministers, Parliament, and the National Development Planning Commission to enable them to track the desired national employment outcomes. This process would require setting up monitoring and evaluation systems at the different levels of programming, completing development and operationalization of the Ghana Labour Market Information System (GLMIS), upgrading public employment centers, and establishing impact measurement mechanisms to regularly evaluate programs for value for money. With support from the Employment Sector Working Group, MELR would have a key role in minimizing duplication of effort and ensuring positive employment outcomes for Ghanaian youth. Finally, the ministry would require adequate human capacity at both the national and local levels to effectively carry out all these responsibilities.

Meanwhile, a comprehensive database on the categories of youth should be put in place to facilitate planning to aid in the design of programs appropriate for each youth category proposed in this study.

Finally, regular interaction among key stakeholders in the youth employment sector is important for promoting synergies, reducing duplication, and sharing knowledge. Private sector involvement, as described in the next section, is critical in these interactions.

LEVERAGING THE PRIVATE SECTOR THROUGH PUBLIC-PRIVATE PARTNERSHIPS

The importance of private sector participation in youth skills development and employment cannot be overstated, even though including private sector employers inevitably adds layers of complexity. Private firms operate under diverse models and may have different motivations for supporting youth employment programs, whether to increase their own productivity and profits or to help ensure that the country has an adequately trained workforce for the long term, or for a combination of these reasons. However, it is critical that the government allow the private sector to take a lead role in youth skills training, and it should provide an environment that encourages private employers to hire youth. Research indicates that training interventions should closely involve employers to ensure that programming is demand-driven (Glick et al. 2015).

Besides helping to shape youth training and jobs programs, the private sector should be included in national planning for education and employment policy making, with a focus on skills development and the creation of national qualification frameworks. This may be achieved through various public-private partnerships.

Private sector involvement in the promotion of entrepreneurship can take different forms. It may include supporting training programs for youth entrepreneurs as part of a company's corporate social responsibility program; mentoring young entrepreneurs; providing guidance to new business owners, grants or credit for starting a business, or business training services through contracted firms; or including youth-run enterprises in value chains as suppliers or distributors. According to Cho and Honorati (2014), private sector delivery of entrepreneurship training leads to better outcomes.

The private sector could help to ensure relevant training programs by supporting the development of curricula for trainers and national qualification frameworks for skills certification. Moreover, business associations representing small enterprises organized around specific sectors could engage with the government to help in the design of training programs, employment services, and certification initiatives. The private sector could participate as well by establishing incubators that are market-driven to provide advice and technical assistance to businesses-in-training. Once programs are established, private sector participation is important in on-the-job training activities.

EDUCATION REFORM

As stated in chapter 2, Ghana's current educational system is not adequately addressing the youth employment challenge (and the changing nature of work) in terms of equipping young people with the requisite cognitive and soft skills and ethical values they need to thrive in the workplace. It is critical that Ghana reform its educational system so that schools can adequately teach their students effective foundational and behavioral skills. Schools need to prioritize guidance counseling and make services available to students on a continual basis to ensure that they make the right choices, plans, and decisions about their future based on job market information. The Ministry of Education (MoE) is expected to assume oversight of all technical and vocational education and training institutions under the current government's agenda, and so MELR can partner with the MoE to ensure that reforms are geared toward ensuring that youth are employment-ready.

Because of the interface between education and the private sector, the two sides can work together to ensure that young people graduate with the skills needed by the job market and help shape the research agenda in academia. Educational and training institutions should review current programs and integrate in them the relevant, demand-driven technology and research that increase youth employability. Education reform should be directed at optimizing career guidance, which can help young people explore options in their areas of interest and, in doing so, indirectly promote talent development.

YOUTH ORIENTATION

The general attitude in Ghana toward employment will have to adapt to an ever-changing global system. Currently, the country's educational system prepares students mainly to look for formal wage employment. Young people tend to have a negative perception of skills-based occupations acquired through apprenticeships and formal technical and vocational training programs, and of agriculture. Although the Council for Technical and Vocational Education and Training (COTVET) has gradually been changing this perception, negative perceptions persist. The government must make a conscious effort to reorient people's thinking so they understand the potential benefits that skills training and entrepreneurship development offer to both individuals and the nation as a whole.

GENDER MAINSTREAMING

According to the *2015 Labor Force Report* (Ghana Statistical Service 2016), in Ghana the female unemployment rate is higher than that for males in all regions except Greater Accra (13.3 percent, females; 15.6 percent, males) and Brong Ahafo (6.8 percent, females; 10.1 percent, males). Female youth unemployment in Ghana is highest in the Ashanti region (15.1 percent), and higher proportions of females (39.0 percent) are engaged as service or sales workers than males (13.9 percent). Furthermore, females tend to not work in agriculture or fisheries, despite the numerous opportunities in these sectors. This tendency could be addressed using inclusive business incubation models.

Young women in many countries face a number of constraints in terms of work. Barriers include household responsibilities, lack of access to education and health services, social norms, and lack of public safety. Social norms also tend to influence choices made by young women; many tend to settle for self-employment in socially acceptable work—such as buying and selling small goods, hairdressing, and catering—that would not jeopardize their social standing. As a result, women are more isolated and have fewer chances to develop the aspirations, skills, networks, and confidence needed to find productive employment. Although countries have made great progress in advancing the education of young women, educated young women are still at a major disadvantage in the formal labor market. They often lack the kinds of education and skills needed for many jobs. As a result, they engage in low-productivity work that affords flexible time commitments. These jobs pay less and tend to not offer benefits such as health care.

Consultations with stakeholders also confirm a gender disparity in youth employment in Ghana. In rural areas, it is particularly difficult for young women to translate their labor into paid work and move from paid work into a stable form of earning. This situation is attributed to the marital and household constraints affecting most women. They are limited in their ability to take advantage of economic and entrepreneurial opportunities because of a system of property rights that is mostly biased against female inheritance and ownership of land and other assets. Furthermore, many women are held back by stereotypes and tend to avoid sectors that are male-dominated (such as construction). Youth employment programs therefore would need to embed incentives to encourage women to take up professions in more male-dominated sectors.

The National Employment Policy, as part of its priority strategies to create more decent work opportunities, intends to promote the development of female entrepreneurship opportunities. Under this strategy, it plans to improve the access of female entrepreneurs to credit, provide adequate institutional support, work to remove cultural inhibitions, and provide practical management training. Continuation of efforts to generate awareness about the importance of female inclusion and gender equality would be helpful as well.

DECENT WORK

The International Labour Organization (ILO) defines decent work as productive work for women and men under conditions of freedom, equality, security, and human dignity. Opportunities for work would deliver a fair income and provide security in the workplace and social protection for workers and their families. The four pillars of the Decent Work Agenda developed by the ILO are (1) employment creation, (2) social protection, (3) rights at work, and (4) social dialogue. In 2015 these pillars became an integral part of the United Nations' 2030 Agenda for Sustainable Development. Sustainable Development Goal 8 calls for the promotion of sustained, inclusive, and sustainable economic growth, full and productive employment, and decent work.

As noted earlier, the main problem in Ghana is not necessarily access to work but the poor quality of the jobs available. Poverty is closely tied to the kind of job a person holds rather than to whether a person works (Honorati 2016). Highly productive jobs are limited within the current dominant informal economy, and opportunities differ for the categories of young people living in rural and urban areas. It is therefore paramount that job creation efforts seek to create decent jobs for all demographic groups.

DISABILITY

Stakeholder consultations highlighted the reality that persons with disabilities are mostly excluded from youth employment programs. The reasons for their exclusion include discrimination by employers toward physically challenged job seekers, a lack of disability-friendly facilities in the workplace, and a widely held view that persons with disabilities are "alms seekers" rather than people who can contribute to national development. Members of this vulnerable group thus face greater challenges in their job search efforts than other populations. In addition, labor market data on persons with a disability are very limited in Ghana. Mechanisms for inclusion are needed in all areas.

TECHNOLOGY

Technology can contribute significantly to a country's market development and boost productivity, especially in primary industries such as agriculture. In Ghana, as in other developing countries, the pace of adaptation to new technologies has generally been slow, even though technology can help raise incomes, create jobs, and boost employment opportunities. Ghana must therefore link its productive sectors and skills development to high technology and innovations that create high returns to investment. Technology and innovation incubators could play a significant role in this effort.

In agriculture, to take one example, the options to leverage science and technology abound. They include input and production technologies for simple farm tools and equipment fabrication, improved seed technologies, greenhouse technology for urban agriculture, small-scale irrigation options for commercial farmers, and aquaculture technology for fish farming. Processing and packaging technologies are notably missing within the Ghanaian agribusiness environment. Other areas in which technology could be utilized are retail and services, construction, renewable energy, and waste management. By developing technology incubators, Ghana could bring on board research institutions to play a role in the transfer of knowledge and in ongoing research projects.

Digital technologies, such as electronic tools and social media, have brought about rapid change in the nature of work. The number of jobs requiring digital skills will grow by an estimated 12 percent by 2024 (Robinson et al. 2018). Thus, to remain attractive to employers, young people must be able to adapt constantly to the rapidly changing demands of firms. Workers will require lifelong learning to acquire skills and knowledge and remain relevant in the labor market. Jobs in the near future will require specific skills—a combination of technological know-how, problem solving, and critical thinking, as well as soft skills such as perseverance, collaboration, and empathy (World Bank 2019). Of particular interest is the impact that digital technologies will have on women, who already are lagging behind men in acquiring education, skills, and jobs. Globally, the proportion of women using the internet is 12 percent lower than that of men; and in almost every region of the world, internet user rates are higher for men. Other factors contributing to the digital gender divide are gaps in information technology infrastructure, the high costs of technology, the lack of relevant content, and the prevalence of online harassment and violence targeting women (Robinson et al. 2018). It is important that youth employment programs address constraints on digital job creation broadly, as well as specific barriers to young women's access to these jobs.

REFERENCES

Cho, Yoonyoung, and Maddalena Honorati. 2013. "Entrepreneurship Programs in Developing Countries: A Meta Regression Analysis." Policy Research Working Paper 6402, World Bank, Washington, DC.

Glick, Peter J., Crystal Huang, Mejia Gonzalez, and Nelly Josefina. 2015. *The Private Sector and Youth Skills and Employment Programs in Low- and Middle-Income Countries.* Solutions for Youth Employment. Washington, DC: World Bank, Solutions for Youth Employment (S4YE).

Honorati, Maddalena. 2016. *Harnessing Youth Potential in Ghana: A Policy Note.* Washington, DC: World Bank.

Robinson, Danielle Simone, Namita Datta, Emily Massey, Tshegofatso Kgasago, Mishkah Jakoet, Peter J. Glick, Diana Gehlhaus Carew, et al. 2018. *Digital Jobs for Youth: Young Women in the Digital Economy.* Solutions for Youth Employment. Washington, DC: World Bank Group, Solutions for Youth Employment (S4YE). http://documents.worldbank.org/curated/en/503651536154914951/Digital-Jobs-for-Youth-Young-Women-in-the-Digital-Economy.

World Bank. 2019. *World Development Report 2019: The Changing Nature of Work.* Washington, DC: World Bank.

7 Conclusions

Ghana's youth employment challenge is vast and requires a multifaceted, deliberate, and consistent response. The government has invested heavily in tackling this challenge, implementing a number of programs aimed at providing skills training and creating new jobs. The private sector has also made significant contributions. However, unemployment and underemployment remain a major problem, and the challenges will only intensify with a projected surge in the country's youth population over the next decade.

A lack of data on youth has hampered efforts to effectively target and address youth employment needs, leading to a fragmented approach. Youth employment programs either overlap or touch only a small percentage of beneficiaries. Job seekers' skills do not match the needs of employers. The country's educational system does not produce versatile graduates, and the technical and vocational education and training system has limited flexibility to allow for innovation and the development of talents. Within existing youth employment programs, there is limited monitoring and evaluation to confirm whether these programs are effective. Within the jobs sector, gender disparities continue to exist: females participate less in the labor market because of various economic and sociocultural factors. Meanwhile, persons with disabilities are mostly excluded from youth employment programs because of discrimination by employers and a lack of disability-friendly facilities in the workplace.

The World Bank commissioned this study to increase the knowledge base on the unemployment challenge in Ghana and provide recommendations for possible ways to address the challenge. Because youth are heterogeneous, the study categorizes Ghanaian youth into six groups based on residency (rural, urban) and education level (uneducated and educated), and it then proposes options tailored to each group's specific needs. Recommendations for investments center on promoting agriculture and agribusiness; apprenticeship (skills training); promoting entrepreneurship; other high-yielding areas, such as renewable energy, construction, sports, and green jobs; and preemployment support services. A focus on these areas can contribute to increasing the productivity of agricultural jobs, grow off-farm self-employment, create more wage jobs, and facilitate the geographical mobility of workers to maximize the benefits of rapid urbanization.

Based on stakeholder consultations and lessons from regional and global studies, this study makes the following recommendations, which can be used to guide the planning and implementation of effective youth employment programs for Ghana:

- *Establish a common database on all categories of youth for use in designing effective programs, targeting the right kinds of participants, and planning such programs.* This effort will require collaboration among those public sector institutions that have mandates for data management and youth employment programming.

- *Strengthen the quality of basic education to ensure that students learn key cognitive and socioemotional skills.* The government has initiated efforts to review the curricula in use at the basic education level. A similar review is needed for the secondary and tertiary levels. Furthermore, skills development programs should upgrade the quality of their services and adapt their content to new jobs that emerge as a result of rapid technological changes and industrialization.

- *Ensure that the current skills training and educational system adequately address the demands of the labor market.* The system also should include more effective preemployment support services, incorporating activities such as internships, job search assistance, and coaching and mentoring.

- *Increase the quality of traditional apprenticeships, which typically absorb junior and senior high school graduates who are unable to further their education.* Such programming requires standard curricula, proficiencies, and certification, as well as modern industry-relevant instructional tools.

- *Partner with the private sector by giving firms incentives to train their staff, involving employers in the design of training curricula, introducing certifications for occupational standards, and encouraging private companies to hire young people.*

- *Introduce systems to improve service delivery and reduce fragmentation and duplication in the employment sector.* These include systems for data management, coordination, and monitoring and evaluation, and they should be in place at both the national and local levels. The Ministry of Employment and Labour Relations would serve as the central coordinator and oversee the production of data needed for decision-making. The ministry could activate the National Employment Coordinating Council and sector working groups as possible channels for coordinating various stakeholders in youth employment.

- *Pay attention to vulnerable groups, including women and persons with disabilities, by introducing specific interventions targeting these groups.*

- *Incorporate technology in both training and on-the-job activities because digital technologies will continue to influence the nature of work.* In addition, ensure that current cognitive and sociobehavioral skills—such as critical thinking, emotional intelligence, teamwork, effective communication, and people management, which are now prominent in the job market—are introduced in youth programs.

Profiles of Youth Employment Programs

PROGRAM	DESCRIPTION
Empowering Novel Agri-business-led Employment for Youth (ENABLE Youth)	ENABLE Youth is a new component of the Rural Enterprises Programme (REP), which was launched in 2017 under the supervision of the Ministry of Trade and Industry (MoTI). ENABLE Youth seeks to create employment opportunities through market-oriented farming and agribusiness. The program focuses on tertiary-level educated youth and youth groups seeking a greater impact within their respective communities and districts.
Ghana Skills Development Initiative (COTVET-GSDI)	Funded by GIZ in partnership with Council for Technical and Vocational Education and Training (COTVET), the Ghana Skills Development Initiative was launched in 2012 and is in its third phase of implementation. The program aims to modernize traditional apprenticeships through an innovative approach to competency-based training (CBT) and by strengthening trade associations and training institutions. The initiative implements its apprenticeship programming using CBT standards and a cooperative training model, combining workplace and school-based training.
Ghana TVET Voucher Project (GTVP)	GTVP is cofinanced by Germany's Kreditanstalt für Wiederaufbau (KfW) and the government of Ghana. It is implemented by COTVET, an agency supervised by the Ministry of Education. The project is the first voucher program in the TVET sector in Ghana and provides competency-based training to both apprentices and their master craftspersons.
Microfinance and Small Loans Centre (MASLOC)	MASLOC is a microfinance institution responsible for implementing the government's microfinance programs directed at reducing poverty and creating jobs and wealth. Over the years, the center has modestly established itself not only as a microfinance institution that disburses micro and small loans to the identified poor in various sectors of the Ghanaian economy, but also as a provider of business advisory services, training, and capacity building for small and medium enterprises. It collaborates as well with institutions to provide them with the skills and knowledge they need to manage their businesses efficiently and effectively.
Nation Builders Corps (NABCO)	NABCO is a special government initiative aimed at addressing graduate unemployment through a structured work and learning program for skills acquisition and development. The program was initiated in 2017 and launched in May 2018 as a special initiative under the Office of the President. It seeks to improve the efficiency of the delivery of certain services within both the public and private sectors. These services include health, industry, education, agriculture, governance, technology, and revenue mobilization. The program places youth in seven structured modules: • Educate Ghana—addresses challenges within the education sector with an emphasis on science, technology, engineering, and mathematics (STEM), and other relevant subjects • Heal Ghana—supports health care delivery across Ghana • Feed Ghana—provides essential services to farmers in e-agriculture and facilitates dissemination of scientific knowledge, mechanization centers, and seed and fertilizer programs • Revenue Ghana—supports revenue mobilization efforts by the Ghana Revenue Authority and metropolitan, municipal, and district assemblies • Digitize Ghana—targets all digitization, innovation, and technology-driven projects in Ghana, including digitization of birth and death records, the National Digital Property Address and Tagging project, and technical and innovation centers. The module also monitors special projects at the constituency level. • Enterprise Ghana—helps private enterprises as well as state-run enterprises and industry-focused state institutions to fill jobs or acquire additional hands to sustain productivity • Civic Ghana—assists at the constituency and district levels with local governance, civic activities, emergency and ambulance services, and projects at the local government level

continued

PROGRAM	DESCRIPTION
National Board for Small Scale Industries (NBSSI)	NBSSI is a government agency established by an act of Parliament (Act 434) in 1981 to contribute to creating an enabling environment for micro, small, and medium enterprises and to deepen the development of an enterprise culture in Ghana. NBSSI manages Business Resource Centres, which are one-stop shops for business development services and currently include the Centers for Excellence for Kaizen in West Africa. NBSSI is supervised by the Ministry of Trade and Industry.
National Entrepreneurship and Innovation Programme (NEIP)	NEIP is a flagship policy initiative of the government of Ghana under the Ministry of Business Development. Established in 2017, the program primarily seeks to provide integrated national support for≈start-ups and small businesses. It mainly furnishes business development services, develops business incubators, and funds youth-owned businesses. Its three main pillars are entrepreneurship, innovation, and integration. The program is implementing four main modules: (1) Business Advisory Services / Business Competitions; (2) Incubation and Acceleration Program; (3) National Entrepreneurship and Innovation Fund; and (4) Agriculture and Industrialization Plan. It envisages creating an enabling environment for the nation's entrepreneurship ecosystem. This program was previously known as the Youth Enterprise Support (YES) program.
National Service Scheme (NSS)	NSS was established in 1973 with a mandate to deploy Ghanaian citizens 18 years and older to undertake national service. The scheme currently deploys graduates of accredited tertiary and professional training institutions to undertake one-year mandatory service in various sectors of the economy. It provides newly qualified graduates with an opportunity to gain practical exposure on the job in both the public and private sectors. The scheme gives user agencies an opportunity to satisfy their human resource needs and gives communities that otherwise would have difficulty participating in mainstream development initiatives access to improved social services through community service provided by national service personnel. The scheme is supervised by the Ministry of Education.
National Vocational Training Institute (NVTI)	NVTI was established by the government of Ghana through an act of Parliament (Act 351) in 1970. The act is supported by Apprenticeship Regulations L.I. 1151 of 1978, Clerical and Secretarial Training Regulations L.I. 981 of 1974, and Trade Testing L.I. 715 of 1971. The institute provides demand-driven employable skills training and seeks to enhance the income-generating capacities of basic and secondary school leavers and other persons. It does this through competency-based apprenticeships, master craftspersonship training, testing and certification, and career development. NVTI has 34 training institutes across all regions of Ghana.
National Youth Authority (NYA)	NYA is a government agency under the Ministry of Youth and Sports that operates under Act 939 (2016). It seeks to develop dynamic, disciplined youth imbued with a spirit of nationalism and a sense of public service. It also formulates policies and implements programs that will promote the well-being of Ghanaian youth. NYA operates 11 Youth Leadership and Skills Training Institutes (YLSTIs), which offer formal skills training (proficiencies and foundational programs) for disadvantaged, unskilled youth in rural communities. The program prepares trainees to test for certifications issued by the National Vocational Training Institute and the National Board for Professional and Technical Examinations (NABTEX). As part of its mandate, NYA also provides short-term, informal skills training (lasting a maximum of three months) and skills empowerment programs for young people in specified areas.
Opportunities Industrialization Centre Ghana (OICG)	OICG was established to contribute to the human capital of Ghana by providing disadvantaged youth with the vocational, technical, and entrepreneurial skills training that would enable them to earn a decent living. OICG was originally established in 1970 to provide skills training to literate, illiterate, and semiliterate youth in Accra, Kumasi, and Takoradi through center-based or formal vocational skills training. The center also provides improved apprenticeship training in more than 18 trades. It is supervised by the Ministry of Employment and Labour Relations.
Rural Enterprises Programme (REP)	REP is part of the government's efforts to reduce poverty and improve living conditions in rural areas. The program's overall goal is to contribute to improved livelihoods and the incomes of rural, poor micro and small entrepreneurs. The specific objective is to increase the number of rural micro, small, and medium enterprises that generate profit, growth, and employment opportunities. The current phase became effective in 2012 as a scaling up of two previous project phases (REP I and II), which were implemented from 1995 to 2011. The program directly supports Ghana's National Industrial Transformation Agenda, anchored on a 10-point agenda, including One District One Factory (1D1F), Strategic Anchor Industries, Development of SMEs, Export Development Programme, and Enhancing Domestic Retail Infrastructure and Made-in-Ghana Promotion. REP is supervised by the Ministry of Trade and Industry. The program works closely with the NBSSI to provide clients at the community level with business development services. It also works with the GRATIS Foundation to deliver technology transfer to businesses and with the Bank of Ghana and ARB Apex Bank to deliver credit to support businesses operations.

continued

PROGRAM	DESCRIPTION
Youth Employment Agency (YEA)	YEA is a public sector employment program established under the Youth Employment Act 2015 (Act 887) and under provisions set out in L.I. 2231. Overseen by the Ministry of Employment and Labour Relations, the program seeks to provide young people ages 15–35 with skills development and training, entrepreneurship training, and employment services support during their transition from unemployment to employment. The program targets the nontertiary-level category of youth and most of the key sectors in Ghana (health, education, agriculture, and security, among others). In 2017 YEA ceased providing support to graduate youth because this function was rolled into the Nation Builders Corps. The program implements the following modules: • Agriculture and afforestation • Community service and security • Sanitation • Community and health assistance • Education (community teaching assistants) • Trades and vocation • Entrepreneurship • Apparel and textiles • Information and communications technology Applicants are selected through a rigorous online process, are matched with one of the modules, and then are enrolled for two years. A monthly allowance is paid by the program.

Source: World Bank.

What Works in Youth Employment
COMPILATION OF GLOBAL AND REGIONAL LESSONS

To better identify what is likely to work in Ghana, this appendix compiles selected findings and lessons from global and regional evaluation studies carried out on youth employment projects. It also highlights some successes in interventions aimed at addressing youth unemployment in Ghana.

WHAT WORKS IN YOUTH EMPLOYMENT?

Evidence suggests that addressing youth unemployment requires comprehensive approaches that tackle both demand and supply factors. In a World Bank Group Independent Evaluation Group (IEG) report evaluating 38 youth employment interventions supported by the World Bank and International Finance Corporation, factors for success included participation of the private sector, monitoring of and follow-up with individual participants, and use of complementary interventions, such as pairing training with job search and placement assistance (IEG 2013). In most cases, a combination of skills development, school–work transition strategies, and interventions to foster job creation and work opportunities tends to be successful. Post-program support services are also thought to be essential to successful interventions. These include mentorship, personalized jobs search assistance, job placement, business development services, and access to credit or grants (IEG 2013).

The evaluation report makes two recommendations: (1) apply an evidence-based approach to youth employment operations, and (2) take a strategic approach to youth employment at the country level by addressing the issue comprehensively through working across sectors with governments and other donors and through stimulating the market environment for growth of enterprises in areas in which youth are concentrated.

A recent report by Fox and Kaul (2017) on strategies for designing youth employment programs in low-income countries suggests that countries need to focus on the structural transformation of their economies. The report questions the effectiveness of supply-side youth employment interventions and makes a stronger case for demand-side interventions that help large firms expand employment opportunities. It also suggests that to increase the number of wage jobs in urban areas, governments need to focus on increasing private investment in the labor-intensive production of goods and services. It is important to ensure that youth enter the labor force with the basic cognitive skills they were supposed to learn in primary and secondary school (Fox and Kaul 2017).

WHAT WORKS IN DEMAND-SIDE INTERVENTIONS?

Structural transformation of the economy lies at the heart of how to tackle youth unemployment and underemployment. Ensuring equitable work opportunities for all requires inclusive growth, so it makes sense to introduce interventions that target improvements in the business climate. However, evidence shows mixed results for programs targeting household enterprises and firms. Support of firms has included helping them to expand (through management training, mentoring, and incubation services); increasing access to finance; reducing business taxation; investing in infrastructure to support firms' entry and growth; and providing employment subsidies to encourage firms to hire youth. For employment, the paramount concern is to create more competitive, productive, labor-intensive enterprises. In discussing how low-income countries can design youth employment programs, Fox and Kaul (2017) note that reducing constraints on firm expansion encourages firms to hire more workers, and interventions directed at larger firms seem more likely to have a positive employment effect.[1] The question, though, is how does one identify the effects of specific interventions on employment outcomes? Table B.1 is a snapshot of the effects of different interventions on wage employment.

TABLE B.1 **Demand-side interventions to increase wage employment**

INPUTS	KEY RESULTS
Access to finance (credit, grants)	*Microcredit:* Studies of demand-side interventions in Bosnia, Ethiopia, India, Mexico, Morocco, and Mongolia revealed positive effects for start-ups, but no employment effects for existing firms. Small loans (US$180–$200) in Uganda also showed no employment effects.
	Larger loans: Subsidized credit and credit guarantees had slightly positive employment effects in Brazil and Colombia, and on larger firms in India. Microenterprises in India saw no employment effects.
	In Nigeria, a *large cash grant (averaging US$50,000)* was awarded to existing entrepreneurs for a business plan competition, with positive effects on employment. Grants in Uganda, which totaled only about US$200 each, experienced low uptake and had no effects on employment.
Financial literacy, business development services, and managerial skills	*High-quality business development consulting,* particularly when directed at developing management skills and when provided by consulting firms, showed positive employment effects in Argentina, Chile, India, and Mexico. Depending on the provider, business development consulting interventions can vary in cost-effectiveness, and many effects may take several years to develop.
	Area of intervention matters: A business development consulting intervention in South Africa found that training focused on marketing and sales produced employment effects, whereas training focused on operational practices and financial management increased efficiency and firm profits without corresponding increases in employment or the wage bill.
	Firm type matters: A business development consulting training intervention in Ghana directed at microenterprises found no employment or earning effects.
Formalization, tax policy	Interventions to increase *registration and business formalization* produce limited results. Simplifying registration processes in Argentina and Brazil resulted in higher formal employment, but the net effects on employment were unclear. Similarly, in other Latin American countries, formalization may have an effect on new or entering firms, but existing firms showed no notable employment effects.
	Paying firms to formalize also produced no effects in Sri Lanka.
	Tax simplification and discounts for microenterprises appeared to have positive employment effects in Brazil and Mexico, although the quality of the evidence was weaker.
Electricity	*Access to electricity* (assessed in terms of quality and quantity) clearly had an impact on firm productivity and growth. A study in Ghana and a model in India both showed positive employment and earnings effects from access to regular electricity. In Ghana, blackouts disproportionately affected employment in smaller firms.
Minimum wage, subsidies, and public works	In South Africa, the introduction of a *minimum wage* created some changes in employment patterns, reducing employment in agriculture and low-paid domestic labor. However, employment effects in other sectors were limited.
	Wage subsidies showed no employment effects beyond the subsidy period in Jordan, South Africa, and Sri Lanka. In Mexico, wage subsidies during a recession increased worker retention and accelerated firm recovery relative to control firms.
	India's *publics works program* (MNREGA) has been successful in increasing employment and earnings in rural areas, with only partial displacement. In Malawi, a similar program found no displacement.

Source: Compiled from Fox and Kaul (2017).

WHAT WORKS IN SUPPLY-SIDE INTERVENTION PROGRAMS?

Training programs tend to be the most common interventions for most youth employment programs. However, the evidence is mixed on the effectiveness of training, which varies in duration and focus and is often provided as a bundle of support aimed at improving youth employability for wage jobs. These characteristics complicate efforts to evaluate such interventions, and results tend to be less conclusive. Nonetheless, some evidence is available for analysis. Results from program reviews in Liberia and Nepal reveal that programs that provided only vocational training had limited results, whereas programs that provided a combination of vocational training, life skills training, and mentoring had positive effects on young women. Comprehensive programs that combined training (vocational or vocational and life skills) with internships or other kinds of work experience showed positive effects in Colombia, Kenya, Nepal, and the Republic of Yemen. Some programs showed positive effects initially, only to have no effects in the longer term. Table B.2 is a summary of lessons learned from evaluations in different countries.

As shown in table B.2, job matching and counseling, job search incentives, and other intermediary support have shown limited positive effects. Similar effects have been produced by providing life skills to increase the employability of

TABLE B.2 Supply-side interventions to increase wage employment

INPUTS	KEY RESULTS
Technical and vocational education and training (TVET), life skills, work experience, or combination	*Life skills-only* interventions in Jordan and Kenya found no effects on employment or earnings.
	TVET-only interventions had no effects on earnings or employment in Kenya or Turkey. India saw slightly positive effects for female employment and earnings, but most likely from displacement.
	TVET and/or life skills together with *work experience* (internship/apprenticeship) *and/or mentoring* showed mixed results by region and gender.
	Positive: Colombia, Kenya, Nepal, Peru, and the Republic of Yemen. *Positive women-only programs*: Kenya (ICT training), Liberia (AGI). *No effects*: Argentina, Dominican Republic, and Peru.
	In Liberia and Nepal, trainers were given financial incentives to place students. Overall, TVET and work experience together seem to have the greatest effects on participation in the formal sector. All studies ignore displacement effects.
	A male-only program in Malawi found that *short-term training in fieldwork plus five days of office experience* increased future employment in temporary jobs.
Employment matching services and counseling	The use of *job fairs* to match job seekers and employers in both Ethiopia and the Philippines noted no significant employment or earning effects.
	Recruitment services targeting young women in rural India for a new employment sector (business process outsourcing) showed positive employment and earnings effects. The novelty of the sector suggests that the recruitment effect may be displacement.
	In Jordan, a *labor market matching service* had no employment or earnings effects and was highly cost-ineffective. Cost per match (assessing ability and fit to job) averaged about US$20,000.
	Apprenticeship matching had a sustained positive employment and earnings effect in Ghana.
Incentives for job search	Interventions testing *bus subsidies for job seekers* found no employment or income effect in Ethiopia, but participants had a higher likelihood of permanent employment due to longer, more intensive job searches. In Bangladesh, a *subsidy to encourage urban migration* during the lean season increased employment and earnings for beneficiaries.
	Although it was not intended to be an incentive for a job search, a *wage subsidy program* in South Africa increased wage employment, even though 98 percent of the firms did not use the wage subsidy. This result suggests that subsidies encouraged beneficiaries to search longer, but the net effect was probably only displacement.

Source: Compiled from Fox and Kaul (2017).
Note: AGI = Adolescent Girls Initiative; ICT = information and communications technology.

young people, yet employers often complain about young people not having employable skills.

Clearly, there is no one-size-fits-all strategy for addressing youth underemployment and unemployment challenges. Nonetheless, it is clear that interventions need to tackle both demand- and supply-side issues. Again, the effectiveness of interventions appears to depend on country contexts, the target beneficiaries, and, most important, the expected end results, which are often wage employment and higher earnings. The definition of a *job* requires further rethinking, depending on the context and what is deemed urgent and realistic for employment outcomes. These global and regional lessons therefore provide guidance on possible options for Ghana based on the outcomes expected from investments.

NOTE

1. This study was not able to undertake an exhaustive review of the literature on this topic.

REFERENCES

Fox, Louise, and Upaasna Kaul. 2017. "The Evidence Is In: How Should Youth Employment Programs in Low-Income Countries Be Designed?" U.S. Agency for International Development, Washington, DC.

IEG (International Evaluation Group). 2013. *Youth Employment Programs: An Evaluation of World Bank and International Finance Corporation Support.* Washington, DC: World Bank.

List of Stakeholders Engaged in Consultative Meetings

MINISTRIES

- Ministry of Employment and Labour Relations
- Ministry of Food and Agriculture
- Ministry of Education
- Ministry of Trade and Industry
- Ministry of Youth and Sports

AGENCIES/DEPARTMENTS/PROGRAMS

- National Board for Small Scale Industries
- Council for Technical and Vocational Education and Training
- Opportunities Industrialization Centre Ghana
- National Vocational Training Institute
- Ghana Education Service, Guidance, and Counselling Unit
- Ministry of Food and Agriculture–Youth in Agriculture Programme
- Rural Enterprises Programme
- Ministry of Employment and Labour Relations–Labour Department
- Youth Employment Agency
- Youth Enterprise Support (YES)-GHANA
- Ghana Social Opportunities Project
- Management Development and Productivity Institute
- Employment Information Bureau
- Advanced Information Technology Institute–Kofi Annan Centre of Excellence in ICT
- National Service Scheme
- National Youth Authority
- Integrated Community Centres for Employable Skills

NONGOVERNMENTAL AND CIVIL SOCIETY ORGANIZATIONS

- TechnoServe
- Christian Aid
- Campaign for Female Education
- British Council

- Enablis Ghana
- African Agribusiness Incubators Network
- Catholic Relief Services
- Local Entrepreneur Skill Development and Education Program (LESDEP)
- Youth Inclusive Entrepreneurial Development Initiative for Employment–Global Communities
- Christian Children's Fund of Canada
- World Education Inc.
- ORIOS Group / GCEEI
- Community and Family Aid Foundation (CAFAF)–Ghana

PRIVATE SECTOR

- Association of Small-Scale Industries
- Ashesi University
- Coca-Cola (5 by 20 program)
- Artisans Association of Ghana
- AGI/X-Solutions
- Impact Hub Accra
- TROTO Tractor
- Kosmos Energy
- AKO Foundation
- Ohumpong Investment Company
- CAS Medical Systems, Ghana

YOUTH NETWORKS

- Agro Mindset
- Gangoyin Youth and Development
- UDS/AGRA Youth in Agriculture Programme
- AFES-GHANA
- Young Professionals for Agricultural Development
- Youth Platform for Africa
- Mumuadu Youth Association
- Passionate Africa Leadership Institute
- Young Enterprise in Farming
- Strategic Youth Network for Development
- Graduate Students Association of Ghana
- Change Leads
- Jerusalem Farmers
- Young Visionary Leaders Ghana
- Ghana Sexual Reproductive Health and Rights Alliance for Young People (GH Alliance)
- Concerned Africans Youth Forum
- Ministry of Food and Agriculture–Youth in Agriculture Programme
- Curious Minds

- The Young Shall Grow
- Bongo Youth Association
- Participatory Development Associates
- Youth Business Network Foundation
- Federation of Young Farmers Ghana
- Youth Advocates Ghana